HERMANN BECKH (1875–1937) studied Law and later Sanskrit, becoming Professor of Oriental Studies at the University of Berlin. A master of ancient and modern languages, he wrote extensively on religious and philosophical subjects, including Buddhism, Indology, Christianity, Alchemy and Music. In 1911, he heard a lecture by Rudolf Steiner and was inspired to join the Anthroposophical Society, where he soon became a valued co-worker. In 1922, he helped found The Christian Community, a movement for religious renewal. His many books are gradually being translated from the original German and published in English.

'From Buddha to Christ' by Katrin Binder

FROM BUDDHA TO CHRIST

(complete text)

With 'Steiner and Buddha: Neo-Buddhist Spiritual Streams and Anthroposophy'

Hermann Beckh

Translated from the German by Alan & Maren Stott
Edited by Neil Franklin, Ph.D. and Dr Katrin Binder

TEMPLE LODGE

Temple Lodge Publishing Ltd.
Hillside House, The Square
Forest Row, RH18 5ES

www.templelodge.com

Published in English by Temple Lodge 2019

Originally published in German under the title *Von Buddha zu Christus* by Verlag der Christengemeinschaft, Stuttgart, 1925

A CIP catalogue record for this book is available from the British Library

ISBN 978 1 912230 25 9

Cover by Morgan Creative
Typeset by DP Photosetting, Neath, West Glamorgan
Printed and bound by 4Edge Ltd., Essex

Contents

Translator's Note

This translation is an unexpurgated version. We have consulted Alfred Heidenreich's severe digest, first published as a series of articles in *The Christian Community Journal*, London 1956, reprinted by Floris Books, Edinburgh 1977. Like Professor Beckh (1875–1937), Dr Heidenreich (1898–1969) was a founder priest of The Christian Community. With Martha Heimeran, he brought The Christian Community to the British Isles (see Alfred Heidenreich, *Growing Point: Story of the Foundation of The Christian Community*. Edinburgh: Floris Books, 1979). His tremendous respect for Beckh was apparent in his lectures and conversation. Dr Heidenreich's example and enthusiasm, as well as that of his colleague Adam Bittleston, have contributed to our re-discovery of Professor Beckh and the impulse to translate the *Collected Works*. Condensed versions of selected passages serve their purpose, but omit much of value. Consequently, as we approach the centenary of the founding of The Christian Community (2022), it is now time to do justice to the full achievement of this Christian priest, Indologist and universal scholar.

In his short but penetrating survey of Beckh's work, Rudolf Frieling (*Hermann Beckh & the Spirit-Word*, Leominster, 2015. 153–60) remarked:

> That *Von Buddha zu Christus* was published by The Christian Community, which was branded as a sect, was probably one of the reasons that hindered it—beyond our circles—from being recognised as an event in the history of European academic studies. But as such it certainly should be recognised.

The full, richly rewarding text is consequently offered here in translation. We have included the Professor's article 'Steiner and Buddha (Neo-Buddhist Spiritual Streams and Anthroposophy)' for its relevance. We are grateful to Dr Gädeke and his colleagues at the Archives in Berlin for a copy of this article. The transcription of the German original (written in old-fashioned Sütterlin) was made by the late Gundhild Kačer-Bock, Beckh's biographer. It was published for the first time in the *Festschrift: Essays in Honour of Hermann Beckh* (in English translation, Anastasi 2016).

Our translation policy to render the author's meaning as closely as possible is the same policy outlined in the 'Translator's Note' to Beckh's major work on Mark's Gospel, as well as elsewhere. In an attempt to be helpful, we have added some sub-titles. We are most grateful to Dr Katrin Binder and Neil Franklin, Ph.D. for editorial help and advice. All remaining shortcomings are mine (A. S.).

Alan & Maren Stott (Stourbridge, 2016)

Preface

In this text one of the possible ways to Christ was to be shown, how this path to Christ can also be sought and discovered from that which was the greatest spiritual impulse of pre-Christian humanity, in which the rich contents of the early Indian spiritual life found once more tremendous expression corresponding to the needs of that time. Blinded by that light which shines out of the East to humanity, many people today lose Christ; following a one-sided guidance pointing to the super-earthly realm, they lose the meaning of the Earth. It should consequently be shown how this search for the super-earthly element can be connected with the meaning of the Earth when the light radiating from the East is penetrated by the light of Christ as the true earthly and cosmic Sun, how through this nothing is taken away from the rich treasures of the pre-Christian past, but only an ultimate and highest treasure is added to them.

Regarding the present composition, there is no intention to give any merely outer, philological teachings about the content of Buddha's teaching. Those looking for such teaching are directed to the author's study *Buddha's Life and Teaching*. These two volumes contain all the essential 'material', as far as the Indian traditions are concerned. Especially the presentation of the Buddha legend in Part I can be mentioned and the presentation of the Buddhist path of meditation in Part II. Everything said in that book about Buddhism is not derivative but drawn from a study of the original texts. Concerning the Christian traditions, in this composition similar things are valid as has already been said in the Preface to *Our Origin in the Light*: it could not have been written had not the author found the light in the spiritual science [anthroposophy] of Rudolf Steiner, which became for him a guide on the path from Buddha to Christ. But in the present contribution the author was striving to work through everything inwardly in an autonomous manner. Reference to anthroposophical writings are given in the footnotes. From the richness of what anthroposophy can say in this realm, only the most important and most essential things could be pointed out.

With this composition, too, the riches of the Christian ritual of The Christian Community could and should be felt as the spiritual background. In particular what is said concerning the great earthly and cosmic question of transformation (transubstantiation, metamorphosis) can add towards an understanding of the Act of Consecration of Man, the Eucharist service of The Christian Community.

Hermann Beckh
Stuttgart, Advent 1925

I.

The Tree of Knowledge and the Tree of Life

The character of the two great spiritual impulses associated with the names of the Buddha and the Christ is shown to us in two cosmic pictures. The first is the sacred, leaf-crowned fig tree beneath which, in lonely midnight meditation, India's greatest sage and saint reached the peak of enlightenment, learning of human suffering and how to overcome it. From humanity's sleep of 'not-knowing', he raised himself to the awakened state of a Buddha. The second is the dry wood of the cross on which hangs the lifeless body of the Son of Man. In Buddha there is a highest knowledge that contains the solving of all the formative forces—and in his own consciousness, when he searches deep enough, the spiritual effort of the Indian helps him find these formative forces or *saṃskāras*. In Christ there is a sublime love, which, to use Novalis' phrase, makes death seem a higher revelation of life; a love that finds in death the secret of life and reveals the hidden sources of eternal being. In Buddha there is a knowledge of suffering from which springs a deep compassion for all that suffers through and in existence. In Christ, out of the deepest suffering a new and loving knowledge of the future is born, such a knowledge as today we can only divine. Buddha achieved a victory over birth, Christ a victory over death. In Buddha there is an end, emancipation from the ties of Earth, extinction; in Christ there is a rejuvenation, resurrection, transformation of the earthly element, metamorphosis, or transubstantiation.

The teaching of Buddha is the last and ripest fruit of the early Eastern spirit. The Christ-event appears as the beginning of a new age and a new spirit, as the germ of new humanity and a new world. The message of Buddha was like the last flicker of primeval cosmic wisdom in an age when the capacity for understanding this wisdom was dying out, even in the Indian people, amongst whom it had lasted longest as an ancient heritage. But the deed of Golgotha was like a renewed kindling of an extinguished heavenly light. Buddha was the last of the great teachers and leaders of early humanity. In the time of man's descent he pointed a way of escape. The revivifying of the dying Earth-existence is the work of Christ. In Him begins the re-ascent. He leads the new humanity on the path by which man becomes a collaborator in the renewal of Earth-existence. In Buddha, everything has an atmosphere of *ending*; in Christ, everything begins *anew*. With Buddha we look into man's past; with Christ, into his future. The Christian Easter-thought points us to the distant future of human consciousness, and in viewing Christ Who passed through death, the meaning of the early Mysteries is renewed and rejuvenated.

'Man is something that must be overcome.' This saying of Nietzsche might also be applied to the teachings of Buddha, though indeed in a rather different sense from Nietzsche's. Yet Buddha would never have expressed it in *this* way because, in fact, he never spoke of 'man, the human being' at all. In his day the word 'man' was not by any means felt in its full significance. The whole content of Indian wisdom could be accurately presented without making use of the word 'man' at all. The human being and humanity had become mere pale shadows to the early Indian. Buddha confronts us as one who overcomes that human race, degenerate through its Fall into sin. We see him as the last great initiate able by his own strength to annul within himself the consequences of the Fall.

It is not as a victor over the human race, but as its *perfecter*, that Christ-Jesus stands before us. In Him there descended to Earth that divine prototype of the human being that had been obscured by the Fall of man. Christ became the restorer of lost mankind. Man, who in the beginning of all things was created by the Elohim in the light of the spirit in the primeval beginning, was prevented by the Fall of man from regaining his true earthly reality; he became earthly man when, in Jesus, the Christ entered as a human being into the earthly world. Through Him, man can once more assume the semblance of that image that the spirit-thought of the divine beings had created in primordial light.

The divine 'I' was woven into this image that the human being still carried in his origin in the light. The Godhead that had created him could still say 'I' in him. By reason of this 'I' man was the true 'image of God'. When the divine prototype was obscured in the Fall, that divine essence, man's true 'I' was lost to him. In Christ he is able to find it again. The name 'Jesus Christ' properly understood contains all the mysteries of the human 'I'. Through Him in reality the 'I' is incorporated again into the development of human consciousness. Only through this 'I' does the human being become truly man; he becomes that being that fully distinguishes him from lower levels of consciousness and being.

It is consequently deeply grounded in the development of human consciousness that in the teaching of Buddha, in the same way that the human being retreats in it, the 'I' too plays no role. Concerning the 'I' or self of man, Buddha teaches only that anything, which in the sensory world or even in the higher states of meditative consciousness might be taken for it, is not in fact the 'I' or self. Whether such an 'I' exists or how it may be found, the Buddha has not revealed. The Buddhist path of knowledge does not lead to the finding of the 'I'. If, here as elsewhere, Buddha maintains a negative attitude he has adapted himself correctly to the lament of human consciousness as he found it. For that higher 'I', dreamily experienced as *ātman* by the early Vedic Indians, had gradually been lost to man's consciousness. Enchained by the powers of death, it could be found again only in that which had been united to the Earth and humanity through Golgotha. The initiates and teachers of mankind, who continued to appear throughout the period of man's descent, could not speak about the 'I'; only since the event of Golgotha can it be made known to a humanity whose consciousness is evolving once more in an upward direction.

Bodhi Tree, the *Tree of Knowledge,* is the name given by the Indians to the tree under which, during that holy night at Uruvela on the river Nairanjara, Buddha found the light of knowledge. Before the mind's eye stands the 'Tree of Knowledge' of which the Paradise story tells. Beside it is another tree of Paradise, the Tree of Life.* Because man ate of the Tree of Knowledge before his time and against the divine will, he lost the Tree of Life. The fruit of knowledge became the fruit of death to him. The Tree of Knowledge and the Tree of Life, which before the Fall of man had interlocked their branches in unity, were then wrenched apart in the polarity of opposition. And so man fell victim to the powers of death. From the heights of his origin in the light, he sinks ever deeper into material existence. Ever stronger grows the influence of the death-forces issuing from the Tree of Knowledge, forces whose effect is felt in man's blood. Ever weaker grows the influence of the forces of the Tree of Life. In the earliest, pre-historical most ancient Indian culture, of which there are no documents and which from astronomical reckonings we have to place several millennia before our time, much of the effects of life still existed. The early Vedas and

* Here and in what follows, cf. H.B., *Our Origin in the Light,* Chapter 3.

Upanishads originate much later but contain an echo; the divine Tree is glorified with its roots in heaven and its branches bowing to the Earth. This sacred fig tree is called *aśvattha,* in which the immortal life of the gods is manifested, and the healing herb *kuṣṭha* is found.[*] In the early Vedas this sacred fig tree is seen as the Tree of Life. 'It is light, purity, immortality, *brahman.*'[†] Those who are called as 'Brahmins' to carry the forces of priesthood in early India and carry on the tradition felt in themselves *brahman,* the divine life in the sacred word, the spiritually creative, magic power of the word. The ancient Indian Yoga is an endeavour to master the forces of knowledge by the breathing, thus renewing the union with the forces of life. In the tree of the blood,[‡] branching out from the heart to all parts of the threefold human organism, the Indian yogi saw the secret of the interlacing and metamorphosis of the Tree of Life and the Tree of Death.

Yet as time went on the old forces grew ever weaker; the Tree of Life withered ever more. Only a scanty residue persisted into the age when Buddha lived and worked, 500 years before our era [CE], the epoch in which those forces reached their lowest ebb. Brahmanism was in deep decline. Buddha brought a kind of religious and spiritual renewal to meet this decline, but he could not restore the abundant fullness of life and wisdom that had characterised the ancient world. The strength of the Tree of Life had waned; man's evolution had led him to the death-fruit of knowledge. It is as the Tree of Knowledge that the sacred fig tree now confronts us. We find it as the Tree of Knowledge with Buddha. But this knowledge, which robbed man in Paradise of his innocence by his plucking this knowledge prematurely, taught him to recognise good and evil. This knowledge divided him from the divine life, entangling him in sin and leading him into the forces of death reigning on Earth. We find with Buddha this very knowledge raised into the most lofty, crystal-clear purity, and to a full understanding of man's Fall into sin, of its cause and its conquest. (What Christians call 'the Fall of man', or 'Fall into sin' was to Buddha the *fall through error into the suffering of the world.* It is true that Buddha never actually spoke of 'sin'; he spoke of what has its origin in 'not-knowing', of the passionate desire that creates suffering.) *Knowledge that entangled man in earthly bonds became a knowledge which frees him from those bonds.* So pure

[*] Atharva Veda, 19, 39.

[†] Kathaka Upanishad 6, 1.

[‡] Ibid, 6, 16.

is this knowledge that, objectively, it has always appeared to earthly thought as 'nothingness', just as pure, clear water in a pure, bright crystal vessel seems 'nothing' to the sensory eye.

This knowledge is not theoretical. Buddha's knowledge was developed by meditation; it penetrated to the foundation of being. Through this knowledge, such a vision is obtained of the effect of the Fall of man on the forces of life in the depths of consciousness, that by it the axe is laid to the root of existence itself. There is something unique, something prodigious in a knowledge that makes him who gains it by meditation master of the very forces of life and existence. Through this the whole deeper meaning is revealed of the picture presented by the Buddhist legend. This says that in the night when Buddha found his knowledge, the Tree of Knowledge burst forth again into luxuriant foliage. Nevertheless, what Buddha found under the sacred fig tree was not yet the real conquest of death, although this expression too is found in the Indian sources. It was not yet the true transformation of the Tree of Death into the Tree of Life. What was attained by Buddha's lofty knowledge was only the last decisive answer to the question asked by the early Indians throughout the ages—what must I do to escape from reincarnation, from the repetition of earthly life, of earthly suffering and of earthly death? How am I to acquire in practice the art not to be born? Only the greatest saints and sages had the power, through meditative energy, to call up that knowledge from the depths of consciousness, in such a form as would really touch the roots of existence. According to tradition, when Buddha found it he spoke the triumphant words: 'House-builder, you are discovered. Never again will you build the house.' As a 'house-builder' there appears to him those powers, which out of the force of the etheric body build the physical body, those powers which in the more abstract terminology of the Indian Sankhya philosophy and Yoga philosophy, also in Buddhist writings, are called *saṃskāras* (Pali *sankhāra*), 'formative forces'. By this they meant the formative or fashioning forces of the subconscious, which bring man into earthly existence, into incarnation, and which the yogi then bring under the control of his consciousness.

In Goethe's *Fairytale*[*] these forces of being are recognised as the Ferryman, who brings the soul out of the land 'beyond the stream', from the spiritual world, over into the earthly physical existence, the

[*] Goethe, *The Green Snake and the Beautiful Lily* (1795), tr. Thomas Carlyle (1832), http://wn.rsarchive.org/RelAuthors/GoetheJW/GreenSnake.html

same forces which in Steiner's mystery drama *The Portal of Initiation* appear as the Spirit of the Elements. The Ferryman's 'hut' is also mentioned in Goethe's *Fairytale*. Only the concern here is not, as with Buddha, with the mere destruction or annulling of the house, the hut, but with the rise of the Temple from the depths. The hut is first broken apart, and then appears as the silver altar in the Temple which is raised above the Earth.

No destruction but *transformation* takes place before us here. In this transformation, the physical element experiences here a *resurrection* into a higher, purer, more etheric form, which unlike the earlier form is not subject to mortality. And so in the pictures of Goethe's *Fairytale* the thought of the Christian resurrection is meaningfully expressed, the same thought of the resurrection or transformation that Paul connected to the picture of the *hut*, or *tent*, when, in 2 Cor 5:4, he says, 'For while we are in this tent, we groan and are burdened, because we do not wish to be *unclothed* but to be *clothed* with our heavenly dwelling, so that what is mortal may be swallowed up by life.' (Similarly 1 Cor. 15:51, 53: '... we will all be changed ... For this perishable must clothe itself with the imperishable.') The deepest and at the same time most pictorial expression in the thought of transformation of the physical element is to be found in the pictures of the Apocalypse (especially chapters 21 and 22). In the changed new Earth descending out of heaven, the 'New Jerusalem', we also find *ξύλον ζωῆς* (Rev. 22:2), which Luther (1545) translates as '*Holz des Lebens*' (literally, 'wood of life'). This is nothing other than the '*Tree of Life*', lost in Paradise, now won again through Christ, in which the perishable is clothed with the imperishable; the Tree of Death has been transformed into the Tree of Life, or is swallowed up by it.

This leads us back to the starting point of our considerations. To that transformation of the Tree of Death itself into the Tree of Life, which first took place on Golgotha, Buddha was not yet able to attain. To escape from death and the repetition of death in future earth-lives, Buddha eliminated reincarnation. This is attempted by everyone who truly follows Buddha's path. He is bound to sever himself from the Earth and humanity, and from their further evolution. And so the Tree of Knowledge, under which Buddha found such sublime enlightenment, has still remained the Tree of Death. The sacred fig tree, which stood resplendent in foliage at the time when Buddha gained his knowledge, spiritually seen, is the same fig tree which withered 500 years later, when Christ pronounced over it the words, 'May no one ever eat fruit from you again' (Mark 11:14). Buddha himself had also foretold that his knowledge and teaching would only truly live for 500 years among human beings.

As the moment of the Mystery of Golgotha drew near, the germinating forces of the Tree of Life, which for Buddha had become merely a Tree of Knowledge, had altogether withered from among men. The dry wood of the cross is a symbol of what the Tree had become. The external eye sees nothing but the dry wood and the lifeless body hanging on it. Spiritual vision sees Christ shining, the Sun-being radiating love; life-giving fresh verdure out of death. The ancient saga* of inexhaustible depths tells how Seth buries three seeds of the Tree of Life in Adam's grave. Out of these seeds there grew a tree; out of its wood wonderful things were fashioned, and finally the cross on Golgotha. Nowhere during the whole course of earthly development have brighter forces of light and love of the Sun shone down into darker earthly depths and depths of consciousness than on the cross of Golgotha. In the cross on Calvary the Tree of Death becomes again the Tree of Life. The waning forces of physical knowledge, the death-forces themselves, become constructive, creative, etheric forces of life. The spiritual Sun-ray that shone from the cross on Calvary penetrated also into the depths of consciousness where Buddha came upon the secret of the formative forces of being. For Buddha this secret could only mean that the axe was laid to the root of existence and of reincarnation, whereas for the Christ this re-creation of the Earth, this permeation of earthly death with the Sun-forces of life, signified lordship over the formative forces of being and resurrection.

At the nadir of existence where Buddha found an end, there was for Christ a *beginning*. The consequences of the Fall of man could not be obliterated by the mere annihilation of earthly existence; only through a re-creation of existence could man grow up again to the image of God that had been obscured by the Fall. The Fall of man must be overcome, not for the individual alone, but for humanity and the Earth.

But now, *has* it been overcome? Is mankind really on the up-grade? Is it not more deeply than ever entangled in sin and suffering, in all the powers of darkness and chaos? Had not ancient India, even in the days of Buddha, a much deeper quest of the Spirit, a much deeper spiritual understanding, a much deeper spiritual culture? Were not human souls more inwardly harmonious at that time? Was not the whole of life

* *Cf.* H. B., *Our Origin in the Light*. Germ. ed. 35.

much more rhythmical? Here we need a penetrating thinking which will look at the facts and also the deeply underlying scheme of things. In the current of time the early Indian lived more in the etheric human nature, surrendered as if in a dream to the great rhythms of the universe. The age of Buddha, because it represents a descent, an end, is characterised by a certain ripeness, indeed an over-ripeness. It suggests the ripeness of a mature fruit, ready to fall. With Christ there came the epoch-making entrance of the spiritual 'I' into the evolution of the Earth and humanity; man's consciousness, the whole configuration of the human soul, experienced the most radical of all changes. Everything stands under the sign of a new beginning, a revolution, a crisis. Closely connected with the evolution of the 'I' are all the difficulties, oppositions, conflicts—all the birth-pangs of the new age with which he is wrestling today, and with which he will indeed have to wrestle in the future to an ever greater extent. The sombre magnificence of the pictures seen by the prophetic eye of the writer of the Apocalypse gives us an idea of the mighty crises that the full acceptance of the Christian 'I'-impulse will bring to mankind.

That impulse of Christ was not taken up by humanity in some kind of conscious understanding. Even the wonderful profound teaching of ancient gnosis, prematurely extinguished, was still connected to certain early forces of consciousness originating from the time of the descent of humanity. It was still far removed from a true understanding of the new element that appeared in Christ.* And what came after it as ecclesiastical development in the West was even more removed from understanding. The facts of church history, in their way significant, prove that a deep effect proceeded from the events in Palestine. In the historical facts, here as everywhere, many of the effects of the events of Christ's life are evident that have entered the earthly stream through the great event of the turning point of time. The actual understanding of what had happened at the turning point did not actually live in the individual human souls, not even in the leading personalities in the development of the Church. Today, too, this understanding does not yet live to a great extent; the Christ-impulse is not actually taken up, not yet fully divined in its essence by individual human souls. Although connected with the Earth and all the events of humanity as a real fact, precisely because it is not at all understood and taken up by

* *Cf.* Rudolf Steiner, *Christ and the Spiritual World*, Leipzig 1913 [GA 149], lecture 1. (For Steiner's works online: rsarchive.org)

the individual human soul, or only in the smallest part, disharmonies from this Impulse proceed from human souls under which they have to suffer so much today. In its unconscious depths the human soul sees itself confronting a power with which pre-Christian humanity did not have to reckon in this way. It finds there the archetypal picture of the human being that had been lost through the Fall; it has to be wrestled for again. Admonishing, this Christ-picture stands before the soul even if the soul is not conscious of this fact. What is not raised out of the hidden depths into consciousness has a tormenting effect.*

The objective influence of Christ on the Earth and humanity—which at the same time is an influence into the unconscious *depths* of each individual person—is to be carefully distinguished from the other question, how much the individual soul consciously realises the impulses of Christ. Right into the life of humanity, in literature, art and science, it could be shown how Christ also works in these realms where the individual poet, artist and scholar has taken up none or few of His impulses. The whole existence of modern natural-scientific research—although at first still materialistic, that is, consequently not penetrated by Christ, can only be understood in connection with certain facts of the development of human consciousness, which again, in a decisive way are presupposed through the impact of the Christian impulse on the evolution of the Earth. In pre-Christian humanity this natural science could not exist in this way; on the other hand, we see the separation of objective Christ-influences and subjective Christianisation clearly in the example of certain religious personalities or religious-mystics, such as Meister Eckhart in the thirteenth century.

Something thoroughly great and spiritual lives in the writings of Meister Eckhart—one may think, for example, of the treatise on solitude†—lives in the whole tone of his words, of their power and inherent holiness. A certain something in these words could never have been expressed by Buddha or any Indian mystic or pre-Christian

*The concept outlined here is revealed as the deepest underlying motif of the Parsifal story in Beckh's study *The Parsifal Christ-Experience in Wagner's Music-Drama*, and again is studied in detail in the author's expositions on *Mark's Gospel: The Cosmic Rhythm* and its sequel, *John's Gospel: The Cosmic Rhythm—Stars and Stones*—Tr. note.

† English translation in *Meister Eckhart, The Essential Sermons, Commentaries, Treatises and Defence*, tr. and ed. by Bernard McGinn and Edmund Colledge. New York: Paulist Press, 1981. Modern scholarship questions Eckhart's authorship of this work—Ed. note.

philosopher. The fact that Christ has connected Himself with the Earth sounds through the tone of Eckhart's words. In Eckhart's conscious 'I', or of those spiritually related to him, the impulse of the Christ Who calls us to be co-creators in the rejuvenation of earthly existence actually does *not* live. Only that impulse lives in his consciousness which turns completely away from the earthly element, and only lives in his own being. But this impulse is not the Christ-impulse, as understood here, but none other than the impulse of *Buddha*—if we disregard the outer Indian framework of Buddha's teaching and only look at what Buddha wanted in the depths of his being. And any deeply religious, even an outwardly Christian religious striving, according to its inner being, can be rather Buddhist than Christian. Our whole present age is rich in Buddhism in the sense meant here. Amongst spiritual seekers, especially in the context of theosophical strivings, many things can be found in this way. Many people today look towards the Far East in order from there to receive the light. The fact is significant that since the nineteenth century an Indian, predominantly Indian-Buddhist, renaissance has come about in Western spiritual life. Hereby the emphasis of the demand lying in the words 'from Buddha to Christ' has to be felt in its earnestness and depths with regard to the inner advancement, in the sense of true progress, meant here for the striving soul.

The true Christian impulse is missing in many things that outwardly appear Christian. Similarly, it can be especially present where it is not apparent to the observer looking at the outer appearances. For example, in Goethe, with whom some have doubted his Christian belief, there lived, in the whole way he thinks, writes and researches, much of that which leads to a direct, further development for the renewal of the dying Earth existence, and in this respect carries Christian impulses in itself. The physical thinking of natural science of today that has become abstract, and only understands the dead mineral element, has been lifted again in Goethe's thinking and researching into a living thinking, a feeling towards the etheric, living element, conceiving the living element—consequently, something like Goethe's *Theory of Colours* cannot be grasped with the scientific thinking still common today. Dead thinking and knowledge then become a shining living thinking, as in Goethe's *Fairytale*, when the Green Snake takes up the gold of wisdom strewn about by the Will o' the Wisps (of academia today), transforming the dead gold into living light through which it becomes transparent and shining.

Re-transformation, not yet achieved by Buddha, was achieved by Christ. What was presented above in a supersensory picture of the re-transformation of the Tree of Death, of Knowledge, into the Tree of Life, or was also presented as the entwining of the two trees, this, in the manner of Goethe's thinking, so different from today's natural scientific thinking, is at least present in seed-form, yet in a tangible form. Goethe himself presents the picture of the Tree of Death entwined again with the Tree of Life in his poetic fragment '*Die Geheimnisse*' as *the cross entwined with roses*. In the picture of the rosy cross Goethe beholds life freshly germinating out of the depths of death. And in the pictures of his *Fairytale*[*] there wholly lives the thought of the shared work and building of the great Temple of the future of humanity, drawn out of the depths of the Christian impulse. This gathers the forces of humanity to a great harmony, hitherto still striving apart; it brings the lost archetypal picture of man again into the light of day, first seen in subterranean depths and lost through the Fall. The deepest Christian impulse lives in Goethe's *Fairytale*, although the word 'Christ' does not once appear in it.

One can say the same about Novalis' fairytale in *Heinrich von Ofterdingen*.[†] On a higher level, still pointing further into the future of humanity, in pictures of truly apocalyptic depths, the Christian thought of the purification and transformation of the earthly element is placed before us, of the re-enlivening of the earthly element through what comes down from above, the tremendous thought of resurrection and transubstantiation. This thought, not taken up into Buddha's impulse, only became reality in Christ. One of the great leading spirits is speaking to us here, one who points the path for humanity's future understanding of Christ. For a mere Buddhist feeling seeking wisdom in a Buddhist sense, the pictures of that fairytale would be empty fantasy.

This objective vision of the Christ-event on the Earth and in humanity, to be differentiated from the conscious reception of the Christian impulse in the human soul, is shown in a very remarkable way by the evolution of Buddhism itself. It has been mentioned that Buddha prophesied that his teaching would not remain unaltered after 500 years, that is, not beyond the great turning point of time. And it was actually about that time that Buddhist thought did change its original

---

[*] See footnote 5 above.

[†] Klingsohr's fairytale is told in Chapter 8 of Novalis' novel *Heinrich von Ofterdingen*.

form and so became a leading religion in Asia. With this Mahayana Buddhism, as it was called, there entered the teaching of the 'Way', or the 'Greater Vehicle', which stressed collaboration in the emancipation of mankind instead of mere individual self-emancipation, the earliest possible escape from the round of reincarnation. So work for the mission and the progress of mankind had begun, although in a definitely Eastern form. In this sense a 'successor to Buddha' is spoken of in the Mahayana, one who did not desire emancipation from reincarnation for himself alone, but who wished to show humanity the way to salvation. We cannot speak of a conscious understanding or conscious acceptance of the Christian impulse in Mahayana Buddhism, nor did this new phase of Buddhism attain to any conscious visualisation of the event of Golgotha. Yet, in this alteration of the fundamental tenets of Buddhism wherever individual thought gives place to cosmic thought, the event of Golgotha is at work. Quite independently of religious creeds, the Mystery of Golgotha is a universal earthly fact. This has not passed through human consciousness and thinking anywhere without leaving some trace. The great revaluation of all values brought about by the deed of Christ also affected the spirit of Buddhism.

In the sacred fig tree under which Buddha found the path which was to lead to freedom from reincarnation, we recognised the Tree of Knowledge which for mankind had become the Tree of Death. This Tree, which was still in luxuriant foliage when Buddha acquired from it the final decisive knowledge, in the spiritual vision of the future is seen to wither, shrivel and die. (Similarly, in Nordic mythology and Wagner's *Twilight of the Gods*, Yggdrasil, the cosmic ash tree, withers away when Odin has taken from it eternal knowledge, the spear of the runes.) By contrast, beneath the dry wood of the cross of Calvary, spiritual vision sees the Tree budding afresh into the future. Turning our eyes to the cosmos, we can also see these forces of the Tree of Knowledge and the Tree of Life in the figures of the Moon and the Sun. There is a lunar character in the whole spiritual life of India that always looks on the fact of birth taking place through the powers of the Moon in the physical world. The Indian then intends to cut himself off from this, but wants to do it in such a way that he as it were returns into the pre-birth sphere. This Moon-sphere is that out of which birth takes place, and now should no longer continue. Such a lunar impulse also lives in the great knowledge of Buddha.

A Sun-impulse lives in the deed of love on Golgotha, which in the depths of death allows life to spring forth anew. This Sun-impulse lives in the entire Christian renewal of the Earth and of humanity, in the process of the Earth becoming Sun once again. In the reflecting, mirroring effect of the moonlight we can sense the essence of knowledge that is connected to declining forces of death; in the sunlight life-awakening strength is at work. The Indian himself speaks of the 'moonrise of knowledge'. And if we look at the sky when the Sun is sinking below the western horizon just as the full Moon is rising in the east, we have a picture of the extinguishing of daylight and day-consciousness of the Earth in the rise of Buddhist knowledge. If we look at the external sunrise in devotion to Christ's deed on Golgotha, we experience the light of Christ in our own daylight. We then recognise a spiritual sunrise for humanity in the Christ Event.

In this simile only *one* of the possible viewpoints is shown. It is the viewpoint which arises when we view the contrasts between Buddha and Christ. But we may also consider how near in time and spirit Buddha stands to the Christian era. Buddha was the last of the really great initiates and teachers of humanity before this moment in time. He leads man's consciousness down to the nadir, from which Christ leads it up on the other side. In many respects Buddha appears as a forerunner, already illumined by the light of Christ. This is expressed in the pattern of his life as given in the details of the Buddhist writings, and also in his doctrine, in particular where he appears before the world proclaiming compassion and love. *Compassion* takes the foremost place, according to the character of the Buddhist knowledge of suffering. But Buddha also speaks with warmth of love, the kind friendliness towards all beings that is radiated in meditation to all directions under heaven. This appears especially in the famous eulogy of love in the Itivuttaka,* which has always been felt as foreshadowing Paul's Christian song of love in I Corinthians. We are told in the Pali text that love, the emancipation of the heart, absorbs into itself and outshines all works of external piety, as the light of the Moon outshines the starlight, or as the Sun, rising at the end of the rainy season in a clear autumn sky, puts to flight all the darkness of the empyrean, or:

> as, when night is ended, the Morning Star shines and gleams and glitters in the early morn, so love outshines all external works of piety. Love, the liberator of the heart, absorbs them within itself and shines and glows and gleams.

* *Itivuttaka*, one of the Pali texts of the collection 'Khuddakanikaya' of the Sutta-Pitaka.

These words had a tremendous significance in the wide realms of Earth to which they were directed; no one had ever yet spoken of love like *this*. Now, through Buddha, a first preparatory but most significant step for the Christianisation of human consciousness was already taken at that time.

It is significant that in this passage as well as in other similes of Buddha, the Morning Star, more even than the sunlight, is given special distinction. As the Morning Star shines before sunrise, the whole of Buddha's message is a preparation for the Sun of Christ. With this the other viewpoint is given that helps us to sense the spiritual element of Buddha and of Buddha's teaching out of the spiritual element of the Morning Star. In the same way we sense the spiritual nature of Christ out of the spiritual nature of the Sun. The Indian word for 'Buddha' (in Buddha's Magadha dialect: *Budha*) clearly expresses this relationship. For *Budha*, closely related with Buddha in its derivation,* means among other things the planet Mercury (in the early teachings always substituted for Venus). Buddha's mother was called Maya, as the Roman Mercury is also the son of Maya.

Between Buddha and Christ we feel not only the contrast but that which in the one already points to the other. With Christ not only a new beginning is placed where something is drawing to its end, but what has become old in the pre-Christian era appears rejuvenated in another form in the Christian era. The ray of Christ's light penetrates right into the furthest distant primordial past of humanity and the Earth, in order to bring humanity's past back to life on a higher level shone through by the strength of the 'I', in humanity's future. In the future great teachers of humanity will appear—called by the Indians Buddhas and Bodhisattvas—who will proclaim to humanity the impulse of Christ. In the midst of the past and future Buddhas stands the spiritual Christ-Sun, radiating its light to them all. Consequently, it is especially significant if we do not remain with external, ecclesiastical Christianity, but want to take up the cosmic Christ-impulse, not only to look at Christianity against the background of the events in Palestine, but to connect these facts again to the greater events of human development. The primordial Indian period, Zarathustra, Buddha, early Egypt, Assyria-Babylonia, everything beside the early Hebrew culture appears significant in order to lay hold of the Christ-impulse in its complete world-encompassing greatness. All the greatness of the past can in a certain sense appear

* *budha* is the adjective, *buddha* the participle, both from the root √ *budh*, 'to awaken'.

again in a Christianity of the future. What we can feel of the cosmic rhythms of unique spiritual greatness, especially with Buddha, that has given many people today a longing towards the spiritual contents of Buddhist teaching, will be illumined by the light of Christ. It will appear in another form in the future if the Christ-impulse is taken up in the right way. Nothing that has true value will be taken from us through this impulse, but through it we shall receive ever richer gifts.

The phrase 'from Buddha to Christ' expresses more than one view. Not only is an inner advance expressed, a turning to what is contemporary and progressive, implying a certain negative judgment on the earlier stage. The expression also says finding the way to Christ—which of course can take place from various starting points—is also possible from the Buddhist side. Something great and valuable will be gained especially when we approach the Christian element starting from the Buddha. Christianising the Buddha's impulse at the same time broadens the Christian horizon.* Initially, looking at both the Buddhist message and the Christian message can provide an idea of this broadening of horizons.

* This was dimly felt in the Middle Ages in the legend of Balaam and Josaphat (attributed to St John of Damascus, Germ. tr. from the Gk. by Ludwig Burchard, Theatiner Verlag, Munich), which is entirely composed of motifs from the legend of Buddha, but in such a way that everything is turned towards the Christian element and serves to glorify Christianity. Like Buddha, the protagonist of the Josaphat legend is also the son of an Indian king. In the name Josaphat is contained, transmitted through the Arabic budhasaph, the Indian bodhisattva. As in that famous narration of the Bodhisattva's four excursions (H.B. Buddha, Vol. 1, 45) through four meetings—on the first excursion he meets a weak old man, then someone ill, then a dead man, and finally a begging monk standing before him in sublime tranquility—he sees the transience of the earthly element and the value of striving for redemption and comes to the consciousness of the Bodhisattva, Josaphat, too, has similar encounters. As a representative of salvation there appears to him the Christian messenger Balaam, who converts him to Christianity. This linking of Christianity to an Indian context appears quite external, at times even naive. Since the nature of Indian religion is presented in an untrue, distorted picture Christianity, decisive in all sorts of biblical contexts, is presented as a path of salvation that is rather Buddhist in character. At the same time deeper spiritual connections of earthly development shine through in the whole narration of the personality known to us as Buddha becoming Christian. It seems that we have here a document ascribed to John of Damascus inspired by a hidden Rosicrucian source passed down to us in a form that is understandable for the consciousness of the time, appearing to us today as naive. In the way it was passed down it has suffered

Contd.
contemporary distortions. In particular with the name Balaam (Num 22–24; Rev 2:14), related to Bileam, deep mysteries are connected seeming to point to connections between the early Egyptian mysteries and Christian Grail esotericism. Cf. Rudolf Steiner's lecture-cycle, *Mysteries of the East and of Christianity* [GA 144], third and fourth lectures. Berlin, 5 & 7 Feb. 1913.

II.

The Gospel of Birth and Death: The Knowledge of Repeated Lives on Earth and of the Law of Destiny

For decades or still longer, as today, certain points of contact between the story of salvation within the Buddhist texts and the Christian Gospels have been clearly recognised as insoluble problems for outer theological and philological research. Attempts that always look to the sources to solve the problems are insufficient.[*] Here anthroposophy gives the key to understanding by showing the actual mystery of those Gospel stories. With this the question of the nature of those points of contact is answered of itself, that is, from within and objectively, not through an outer literary investigation.[†]

First of all, anthroposophy points out that the cosmic Christ first entered the earthly vessel of Jesus of Nazareth at the Baptism in the River Jordan. Hitherto it overshadowed more from above. The direct embodiment of the sublime Sun-being or another divine being is not seen in the Buddha, but of a high, possibly the highest, initiate in historic time who as such is initially overshadowed by a specific planetary spirituality, Venus-Mercury, and through this was illuminated only indirectly by the cosmic Christ Sun-being.[‡] Ultimately, all the great teachers of humanity, the Buddhas and Bodhisattvas of the past and of

---

[*] This manner of research is found in the otherwise valuable works presenting the whole problem: Rudolf Seydel, *Die Buddha-Legende und das Leben Jesu* (Weimar 1897; reprints: Kessinger 2010, Nabu Press 2014), G.A. van den Bergh van Eysinga, *Indische Einflüsse auf evangelische Erzählungen* (Göttingen 1909), Eng. tr. *Radical Views about the New Testament* (Forgotten Books 2015), Richard Garbe, *Indien und das Christentum* (Tübingen 1914/ 2015), and other writers.

[†] In addition to Rudolf Steiner, *Christianity as Mystical Fact* [GA 8], most important is the lecture-cycle, Basel, 15–26 Sept. 1909, *The Gospel of St Luke/ According to Luke* [GA 114].

[‡] Rudolf Steiner, *The Spiritual Beings in the Heavenly Bodies and in the Kingdoms of Nature*. Lecture 9, Helsinki, 13 April 1912 [GA 136].

the future, receive their light from the central Christ-Sun. The union of the divine cosmic nature, the Sun-being, with human nature meeting us in the life of Christ was a unique occurrence in earthly evolution.

Great teachers of humanity, although appearing between long intervals, have been many. The Indian and all Buddhist traditions emphasise the plurality of Buddhas and Bodhisattvas ('Bodhisattva' is the name of the being destined in a specific earthly incarnation to become a Buddha, through gaining the knowledge of severing the return to earthly life). We are told that the life's course of such a Bodhisattva, leading him to Buddhahood, agrees in all *essential* points with all his predecessors and followers. Outer circumstances can be different, as, for example, that each Buddha finds knowledge under a different tree, not always, as for the Buddha last to appear, under an *aśvattha*, a sacred fig tree, *ficus religiosa*. The lifespan, too, of a Buddha differs in the different ages. The essential thing is that we look through the outer pictures of the legend to the decisive inner spiritual experiences in which the initiation takes place. In this lies the agreement, not the outer situations of life that can indeed be different. For the inner experiences that lead to initiation are always the same, depending on the nature of the matter and the laws of spiritual development. The lifespan of an initiate, as Rudolf Steiner emphasises in his book *Christianity as Mystical Fact* [GA 8], shows a typical character.*

But after what has already been said, the mystery of the life of Christ cannot simply be grasped by looking at Christ as a high human initiate. As anthroposophy confirms, he was precisely something completely different, *incomparable*. With the initiate the human being has developed towards something super-human, towards the divine nature; in Jesus Christ a God Himself became Man. The divine descended into a human vessel. Christ, in Whom the Solar Logos Itself had become flesh, was no mere human initiate. Consequently, his life is also not exhausted in a typical career of an initiate. And yet *certain* points of contact with it can be found in the life of Jesus, as the Gospels tell, especially in the life of Jesus of Nazareth *before* the Christ-being had connected with the vessel of Jesus. In this life of Jesus of Nazareth there radiated already at his birth the Star of the Magi, the Star of Zarathustra, who, beside Buddha, was the other great human initiate in

* A delicate echo of this is contained in a 'Fragment' of Novalis: 'The life of a truly canonical [historical] human being has throughout to be symbolical.'

pre-Christian times.* And from another, beams of the Buddha himself radiated into the life of the child Jesus, before it was illuminated by the Christ-Sun.

So it can be explained that especially the story of the youth of the Christian Saviour, before he became Christ at the Baptism in the Jordan, shows us such a similarity with the Buddha legend. Besides the canonical Gospels the Apocryphal Gospels that are especially dedicated to the Saviour's childhood and youth are important. In their outer appearance the birth of the Saviour is told quite differently in the Buddha legend and the Christian Gospels. Buddha is born as a prince in the palace of a nobleman in a flowering garden in the splendour of spring.† Jesus is born in the poorest place, in a stable. But even in what was here a real outer event, we can see inner spiritual connections as through a *picture*. Buddha is born into a rich inheritance; he belongs to a time and a people that are still nourished by the treasures of the past. The birth of Jesus, which we celebrate so meaningfully in the middle of winter, during the time of the Sun's deepest point in the sky, takes place during a time when humanity had used up the old inheritance of consciousness, with a people that already then to a certain extent was disinherited among the other nations.

Conception and birth

But with all the differences of the outer circumstance, over the manner of this birth the same mystery reigns as that which reigned over the birth of Buddha. Both, as we can say in a Christian religious sense, are the *working of the Holy Spirit*. Not in the sense that the birth took place without an earthly father. For what then would be the sense of the extensive genealogy in Matthew and Luke? Do not these two family trees leading to the father tell us with what care through the generations the divine leadership prepared the earthly vessel that later was to receive the Christ?‡ In the Indian legend it is the spiritual being of the Bodhisattva itself, which from higher worlds, after careful considerations and consultations with the gods, chose the suitable parents for the

* *Cf.* Rudolf Steiner, *The Gospel of St Luke/ According to Luke*, Lecture 4ff. Basel, Sept. 1909 [GA 114].

† H. B. *Buddha und seine Lehre*. Vol. 1. 35.

‡ Rudolf Steiner, *The Gospel of St Matthew/ According to Matthew*. Lecture 3. Berne, 3 Sept. 1910 [GA 123].

earthly birth. Here the qualities of the father were also considered. The working of the Holy Spirit in the birth of Buddha as well as of Jesus of Nazareth, involves that here a conception takes place in such a way that especially with the mother all feelings and urges of a sensual nature arising out of the earthly realm are excluded. She is only conscious of what takes place as a super-sensory event, feeling herself to be but a pure vessel for that which full of grace wants to descend to her out of cosmic heights. What in the Christian Gospels is to be found more behind than in the words is told us in the Indian story in the immediate outer sounds of speech. Especially at this point in the Buddha legend we have a key to understand the Christian Gospel.

The Buddha legend* surrounds the supersensory experiences of Queen Maya before the birth of the Bodhisattva with a fragrant, gentle, transfigured glow. In feeling the influence of the Bodhisattva, who already is in the process to descend out of heavenly heights to the Earth, she directs her longing towards a modest withdrawal, towards a place where no disharmony of the outer world reaches her, no word of strife or anger can be heard in her immediate presence. Bedded on flowers, she rests, given over to beautiful pictures, listening to gentle sounds, breathing sweet fragrances. There she dreams how she is taken up on her bed by the archangels of the four directions of the world to the Himalayas. In the picture of the highest snowy mountains of the Earth she perceives the higher worlds, the world of the ether. Up there she is approached by goddesses who take her to a nearby lake. There she is bathed, all trace of earthly dust clinging to her is removed, then she is anointed with heavenly scents, clothed in heavenly garments and adorned with heavenly flowers. In her dream she then ascends to the 'Silver Mountain', the peak of which is crowned by the 'Gold Palace'. Resting there on a heavenly couch prepared for her by the goddesses she is approached from the nearby yet higher 'Gold Mountain' by the Bodhisattva in the form of a white elephant—the Indian symbol for the highest initiate. The Bodhisattva walks three times reverently around her couch and enters on the right side into her body. The Queen awakes from her dream in super-earthly bliss.

On the one hand, the simple inwardness of the story in Luke's Gospel stands in a remarkable contrast to the dream-lost, earthly transcendent mood of this Indian narration. Mary in all consciousness of her earthly humbleness becomes the vessel for what is super-earthly:

---

*Nidānakathā II, p. 50 of the Jātaka edition of Fausboell, Vol. I, London 1877.

'Behold, the handmaiden of the Lord; be it unto me according to thy word' (Luke 1:38). In this contrast lies much of what is expressed to us in the words 'from Buddha to Christ'. In the earlier story there is the drifting into the super-earthly element so that all the earthly ground disappears, in the later story a simple, humble taking-in of the super-earthly into the earthly situation.

On the other hand, the rich pictorial nature of the Indian legend stands close in time to the Christian era.* In style it is quite different from the early Buddha texts. Thus these texts, lacking in pictures, can be brought into an inner connection to the objective working of Christ in the Earth and in humanity, as characterised earlier. When for the Indian the abundance of pictures had for a long while faded away, with Buddha, at first only in small beginnings, pictures start to arise again in the place of abstraction. Here, too, in the Christian era a whole richness of imagination develops. Through Christ the consciousness of humanity slowly turns again towards pictures. Today, moreover, we still stand at the beginning of this development.

Mary and Maya

The effect of the Holy, the *Healing Spirit*, is expressed in the Buddha legend, especially in the healing forces that proceed from Queen Maya during the time of her pregnancy. Sick people brought to her become healthy when she puts her right hand on their heads, or gives them a blade of grass pulled from the earth. Similar stories are told of Mary, nevertheless before the super-earthly conception, by the apocryphal infancy Gospels (see what is called the 'Gospel of Pseudo-Matthew').† With Maya, and similarly with Mary, there is something of the great cosmic Mother—which in the Indian language is also the meaning of the word Maya. With all the differences in the earthly realm, Mary and Maya are closely related in the spiritual realm. With a glorification of

* The gist of the legend, however, is demonstrably old, only the versions handed down are of a later date. Consequently conclusions cannot be drawn of derivations from Christian sources from these later dates.

† Included in Emil Bock's *The Childhood of Jesus: The Unknown Years*, Edinburgh: Floris Books, 2007, the 'Gospel of Pseudo-Matthew', pp. 225–277; the 'Arabian Gospel of the Childhood', pp. 279–305. The translation in the *Ante-Nicene Fathers*, Vol. 8, 1886. Ed. Alexander Roberts, Sir James Donaldson, Arthur Cleveland Coxe, is available from websites, e.g.: http://www.gnosis.org/library/psudomat.htm/ and http://biblehub.com/library/unknown/the_gospel_of_pseudo-matthew/

the woman, otherwise quite foreign to the Indian, especially the Buddhists, Maya is celebrated everywhere in the Indian texts on the legends, similar to Mary in the Christian tradition, as a picture of noble femininity and virginal purity.*

Already with the descent of the Bodhisattva from the higher worlds, and then again with his earthly birth, the Buddha-legend tells of the immeasurable glory of light that fills all the worlds and the realms between them and penetrates right into the abyss of Hell so that the damned for a moment were relieved of their pain. Sun and Moon paled before this glory of light. With human beings all the lower feelings are silenced; even the animals give up devouring each other; all beings are filled with love and goodwill as fathers and mothers to their children. In the first part of that description we are reminded especially of that which the apocryphal infancy Gospels (this is the 'Gospel of Pseudo-Matthew', Bock 2007. p. 250, with the 'Arabian Gospel of the Childhood'. p. 280) narrate of the glory of light in the cave at the cave of birth, immediately before the birth of the child Jesus:

> There was no light, ever, in this cave. Darkness prevailed always and nothing of daylight penetrated into this cave. But when Mary entered it, the whole cave suddenly shone with a bright radiance. As if the sun were itself within it, so the cave made manifest the whole lightning-force of light. And as if it had turned high noon in it, so that cave was now quite filled with divine light. And this divine light did not leave by day or by night, as long as Mary remained there ...

The Christmas narration of Luke's Gospel tells of the 'glory of the Lord', the glory of the divine splendour of revelation (*δόξα κυρίου*), which during the night in the fields shone around the shepherds. Here, too, the Christian narration again shows us simple inwardness in place of the grandeur in the Indian narrations. In the closest and most intimate manner the Indian and the Christian narration meet through

---

* *Cf.* H. B. *Buddha and his Teaching*. (Göschen, I, 31): 'The mother of the future Buddha has to be adorned by virtues of the highest kind: she has to be of perfect physical beauty, with a smiling countenance, intelligent, without falsehood, not prone to anger, "free from the faults of her sex".' It is said of the young Queen Maya that she stood out from everyone by the smile on her countenance, a beautiful forehead, pleasant voice, perfectly proportioned body, friendly and gentle manner. *Lalitavistara* emphasises that she arose early, similarly it is said of Mary in the Infancy Gospel (Bock, *ibid.*): 'She made it a rule to pray from daybreak to the third hour [9 am].'

these mighty rays of cosmic love. At the Indian birth of the saviour all beings were filled with this, and with the Christian narration it penetrates the hearts of the poor shepherds. In this cosmic love the being of the Buddha reigns, shone all over in higher worlds by the light of Christ. Buddha was indeed the first great teacher to proclaim such an all-embracing love to the people. Here, as we saw, lies the point where we can feel most directly the forerunner of Christ. It is the rays of Buddha, anthroposophy reveals,* that shine into the Christian Gospel in that message of peace and love from the angels [Luke 2:14]:

> Glory to God in the highest, and peace on Earth to men of goodwill.

Journey into Egypt

The apocryphal infancy Gospel (Bock 2007, 63 & 125) tells how Mary on the journey to Egypt enters a temple in the town of Hermes where there were 365 divine images.

> When the most heavenly Mary with her little child entered the temple all the pictures of the gods fell to the earth, so that they lay on their faces, all mixed up, distorted and broken. Thus they clearly proved before the eyes of everyone that in essence they were nothing.

We find almost the same in the Buddha legend,† where it adds that the divine images begin to speak and worship the child. The basic thought is similar in the scene in the school of the Christian story (*The Childhood of Jesus* 76 & 165) as well as the Indian legend, only that the Indian teacher meets the child from the beginning with much greater reverence than the Hebrew one. The child Jesus in the apocryphal Gospel explains the deep meaning of the sounds and the written symbols, pointing us to the mystery of the cosmic word; the Indian legend tells more outwardly how the Buddha-child knows all possible scripts including those that are even unknown to the teacher. With him each sound becomes the initial letter of a word or sentence that later becomes the Buddhist teaching of salvation.‡

If we turn from the apocryphal to Luke's Gospel, which amongst the biblical gospels shows most contact between Buddhism and Christianity, then we find there the main so-called 'parallels' of the child-

---

* Rudolf Steiner, *The Gospel of St Luke/ According to Luke* [GA 114]. Lecture 2.

† *Lalitavistara*, Chap. 8, see H. B. *Buddha's Life and Teaching* (Göschen, I, 39).

‡ *Lalitavistara*, Chap. 10, see *ibid*.

hood story, the well-known narration of the ancient Simeon, who in the Temple takes the child Jesus into his arms. In grateful emotion he recognises in him the future saviour of the world (Luke 2: 25–35). The Indian legend tells us how an old pious seer called Asita, a rishi gifted with supersensory power, saw the jubilation of the heavenly hosts from his hermitage in the Himalayas through the power of the supersensory eye, and on becoming aware of this also saw the birth of the Bodhisattva in the town of Kapilavastu in northern India. He went to the birth-town of the Bodhisattva, and appeared in the palace in order to see the new-born child. The legend tells how he is lifted through the power of yoga into the air and in this way as it were arrives on the 'path of the wind', which was then compared to the Greek ἐν τῷ πνεύματι (Luther translates: '*aus Anregen des Geistes*'—'out of the stimulus of the spirit' [Luke 2:27. NIV 'moved by the spirit']). Not only literal derivation, as outer research has always meant, is the concern here, but deeper connections which especially open up when, besides what is similar, we also consider what is different in the narrations. Like Simeon, Asita, too, takes the child in his arms. He recognises in him 'the signs of the great being' and venerates him. With Simeon everything is grateful joy:

> Lord, now lettest thou thy servant depart in peace according to thy word, for mine eyes have seen thy salvation which thou hast prepared before the face of all people ...

whereas Asita suddenly breaks into tears. The king becomes anxious that the seer had beheld some kind of disaster in the child's future. But Asita answers that he does not cry on account of the child but for himself. Because of his great age he will not experience the day when the child, the present Bodhisattva, will become a world-saviour, a complete Buddha. 'Because, O King, I will no longer behold this Buddha-gem, that is why I weep and am sad in my heart.'

To meet the saviour, the Buddha, was for Asita the main longing of his life. Was this longing ever fulfilled? For the Western person, stuck in everyday thinking, this question can be promptly and obviously answered by a 'No'. Not so for the Indian, the more thoughtful person of the East. Such an observer standing in the Eastern, Buddhist thinking will say to himself: Such a deep longing of the heart, when behind it stands the concentrated power of thinking of a seer and initiate like Asita, carries in itself the seed of its fulfilment. The wheel of rebirth carries in itself infinite possibilities. What, inwardly seeking, could not be found in one earthly life will be met in a later life. For each soul the finding of what it inwardly, seriously seeks is certain. And the all-ruling destiny, *karma,* will determine the moment when this finding is possible. Such a generally applicable answer will be found by a thinking that looks towards Buddha and with this takes up the concept of reincarnation. But with this the concrete, tangible example of the case in point is not yet given.

This tangible answer will only come to someone who is able also to place the knowledge of repeated earthly lives and of the laws of destiny gained from Buddha into the light of Christ, in which the 'I' passing from life to life—yet this [its existence, its nature] is left uncertain by Buddha—will be able to be seen in its individual clarity. In this light of Christ, this person will be able to recognise how those loving rays of the Buddha for which Asita longs, shine more than 500 years later over the child born in Palestine, even before the cosmic Sun of Christ above that child radiates in him, which then the Hebrew seer takes into his arms. From here but one step is required towards the inner vision which finds in the Indian and the later Hebrew the same 'I'-individuality. The longing unfulfilled in the Asita-incarnation finds its fulfilment in the Simeon-incarnation. All unexplained similarities and unexplained differences of both 'parallels' are resolved if we may ask ourselves: was the Indian seer who came to see the Buddha-child, the Bodhisattva, none other than the Hebrew seer, who held the child Jesus in his arms? The Christ governing the cosmic destiny and human destiny had taken in the deep heart's wish of the old Asita and changed the tears of longing in the earlier life into tears of joy and gratitude.[*]

The twelve-year-old

Most clearly of all, this Asita-Simeon story shows how spiritual rays from the Buddha illuminate the childhood of Jesus of Nazareth, before the full Christ-Sun rays forth for him. The agreement is not so clear with the other story, where his relatives miss the child and then find him again in a remote place, in a condition of awakened religious inner life. In the *story of the twelve-year-old Jesus in the Temple* (Luke 2:42–51) his parents find their lost [son] who had remained in the Temple at Jeru-

[*] What is presented here more hypothetically is presented by Rudolf Steiner in his lecture-cycle on Luke's Gospel [GA 114] at the end of lecture 2 as a specific result of spiritual-scientific research.

salem with the group of teachers, to whom he listens and gives astute answers, so that his mother is horrified. Once the Buddha-child went into the country, lost to his companions. He was finally found sitting cross-legged under a Malabar plum tree [*Syzygium jambos*] in lonely meditation, in which he was in supersensory communication with certain sublime cosmic teachers, with the holy rishis. What was said above concerning 'the typical life of the initiate' helps us here to understand several things. Without denying the distant similarity of the events, deeper spiritual research has to point out that actually here not rays from Buddha shine into the life of Jesus, but that other specific contexts are present.*

From the moment when in the Baptism in the Jordan the cosmic Christ, the Sun-being, unites with the vessel of Jesus of Nazareth, we can no longer speak of the life of Jesus illuminated by rays of the Buddha. When later some significant points of contact between the earthly and the Christian Gospel story occur, we can feel that here and there something of a presentiment lights up of Christ in the life of Buddha, that here *rays of Christ* shine into the life of Buddha. We have to remember that the union of Christ with the Earth, before its completion in the Mystery of Golgotha, was prepared for hundreds of years. It was spoken about from the first proclamation of cosmic love in Buddha, which is fulfilled in Christ. The Morning Star, as it is said, announces the dawning of the light of day [the Day-Star]; in these rays of love, however, there shines once more the light of Christ. The Christian experience of freedom can also be shown in a certain way as it is prepared in Buddha. [Through his teaching] Buddha brought the all-moving centre into the human being and into the realm of his inner verdict, even if he did not speak much about the human being. Most clearly perceptible are the rays of Christ descending on Buddha in that early Buddhist narration, which in its style is closest to the Christian Gospels—although this can only be meant as a soft distant echo. This is the narration of Buddha's passing from the Earth, in the Mahāparinibbānasutta of the Dīghanikāya, the '*sūtra* (text) of the great *nirvāṇa*'. It is as if before his parting from the Earth an especially bright ray of the light of Christ had still shone over the Buddha so that already something like a divining of the event of Christ can be found in the event of

*Namely those contexts that point to both Jesus boys (of Luke's and Matthew's Gospels), and the influence of the 'I', or ego, of Zarathustra. Further details in Rudolf Steiner, *The Gospel of St Luke/ According to Luke*, lecture 5 [GA 114].

Buddha. This narration, definitely originating in the early pre-Christian Buddhist era, is especially valuable, for it still reflects the spirit of Buddha's time in a pure form, unlike some of the legend-texts so far mentioned which originate from the Christian turning point of time.

These rays of Christ can already be felt in the whole intimate, sacred way that Buddha speaks once more to his disciples before his passing—although regarding the content the differences from the Farewell Discourses of Jesus are significant. Christ says [John 14:18], 'I will not leave you as orphans. I will come to you' and [Matt. 28:20] 'And surely I am with you always, to the very end of the cosmic age.' Buddha says, 'The teaching which I gave to you is your master when I have passed on.' We feel the rays of Christ playing into earthly history, for example, in the interest that Buddha directs more than usually towards earthly events and the beauty of the Earth in what he prophesies about the future of the then newly-founded town Pataliputra.* With his farewell to Vesali, his favourite town, he throws a sublime, final parting glance towards the beloved place. And then, in that scene with Ambapali, the courtesan/ dancer, who does not surrender the honour of hosting the Buddha even to the noblemen who offer her riches: after he had partaken of the meal with her, she listens in deep devotion to the words of the teacher. Sitting at the feet of the master, she gives him her great park as a present. She can be viewed as a premonition of Mary Magdalene.

With all the differences of the life of Jesus and the life of Buddha, with all the basic differences between the influence of both saviours, there still exists a certain trait in Buddha's influence similar to Christ's. Christ lives for three years in the body of Jesus of Nazareth and then after increasing conflict, as John's Gospel describes so dramatically, is nailed to the cross by the [enmity of] the Jews. The Buddha works even into old age as a spiritual teacher, wandering and preaching, celebrated and venerated by millions, hardly anywhere disputed. Yet, however one attempts to draw comparisons here one will never come further than to that scene of the Transfiguration. This has to be seen as the last great and final parallel between Buddha and Christ. What then followed with Buddha is but his farewell to the Earth, the *nirvāṇa* (more correctly, *parinirvāṇa*). Some kind of connection between this *nirvāṇa*, or spoken from the aspect of the sensory world, Buddha's death, and the

* H. B., *Buddha*, I, 69.

death on the cross on Golgotha cannot be drawn, since this death on the cross, the Mystery of Golgotha, according to its nature is something completely different from Buddha's *nirvāṇa*. Buddha disappears into *nirvāṇa* from the earthly [sphere], whereas Christ through the Mystery of Golgotha connects himself spiritually with the Earth and plants into the Earth the seed for its renewal, its Sun-becoming.* Through Christ's death the dying earthly element itself is transformed; Christ appears to the disciples in a transfigured body, a resurrection body after he had burst the chains of the grave. This mystery of resurrection that is closely connected with the mystery of transformation of the Earth, of transubstantiation, is at the same time that point in which the earthly life of Christ goes in a decisive manner beyond the life of Buddha. Buddha severs birth and disappears from the Earth; he dies for the last time, returning into the realm of night from whence the Mother sent him into earthly existence (the words are to be understood here in a deep spiritual sense); Christ truly overcomes death in His resurrection; He transforms the Tree of Death into the Tree of Life.

The scene of the Transfiguration precedes Christ's death on the cross as it precedes Buddha's *nirvāṇa*. In both cases the process is closely connected with the taking-up into the will of the anticipated earthly death. With Christ it is the loving decision to sacrifice Himself for humanity and the Earth, as related in the three synoptic Gospels (Matt. 16:17; Mark 8:9; Luke 9) in connection to the Transfiguration. With Buddha—after he too had spoken of the possibility of a similar sacrifice to his favourite disciple Ananda yet had met no understanding from him—it is the mere will to discharge the earthly existence and any further connection with the Earth and humanity. 'Then the Holy One released from himself,' says the legend, 'out of his formative forces the *saṃskāra* of life.' This means, he, Buddha, has become master of the formative forces of existence. With this he has the power to hold back life in himself, or also through his pure will to give up this physical life (similar to Christ in John's Gospel 10:18 [NIV] speaking of His life: 'I have the authority to lay it down and authority to take it up again.'). With normal people this power remains unconscious, and consequently is not subject to the will. In one specific, decisive moment of his life Buddha gives to this power standing under his conscious will the

*In a lecture Rudolf Steiner gave in London (2 May, 1913. GA 152), we find the sentence: 'When the Mystery of Golgotha took place the earthly body of Jesus of Nazareth was given over to the elements, and from that time the Christ was united with the spiritual sphere of the Earth and lives in it.'

negative direction; he gives up the will for life. Before he enters *nirvāṇa,* his body radiates once more in a wonderful glory that had already radiated from him on that night when he found enlightenment under the Bodhi tree—a transfigured shining spreads out once more over outer nature, before it succumbs to the winter storms. The narration of the event, as given in Mahāparinibbānasutta, does not by a long way reach the superearthly-cosmic sublimity of the Christian Transfiguration story. The reason for this will be understood after what has been said. The whole deep cosmic connection inwardly connecting the Transfiguration of Christ with the Mystery of Golgotha is missing. Its grandiose expression is in the appearance of Moses and Elijah, the carriers of the two great streams of earthly development* tending towards the Tree of Knowledge and the Tree of Life. Access to these two great streams in such a way that He connects them again through the Sun-radiating power of cosmic love is not yet given to Buddha but to Christ.† This cosmic love is decisively expressed for the whole development of the Earth in the death on the cross of Golgotha; his life and his inner development could not yet lead Buddha to this point.

Buddha's Transfiguration is described in the Mahāparinibbānasutta. From a friendly nobleman he receives a couple of golden garments (or fabric material). Buddha requests that one is laid over him and the other over Ananda. Somewhat later Buddha himself puts on the two garments. At this moment a glorious, blinding snow-white light proceeds from the body of the Holy One, in comparison to which the golden colour of both garments completely pales. Astonished, Ananda asks the Master the mystery of the occurrence. Buddha explains how twice in his life the body of the Holy One would shine in such a manner. Once was in the night when he became Buddha, and then again before he enters into the highest *nirvāṇa.* Christ after His Transfiguration on the mount—Buddha's Transfiguration only takes place in the vicinity of the mountains, but of the highest mountains of the world with their eternal snow—speaks to His disciples of His approaching death on Golgotha. On this occasion Buddha too announces that on that night he would go to Kusinara, he would pass to highest *nirvāṇa* under a twin pair of Sala trees (allowing us to think of the great symbol

* *Cf.* Rudolf Steiner's explanation of the Fourth Seal (Rev 6:7–8) in *Occult Signs and Seals* [GA 284].

† *Cf.* Rudolf Steiner, *The Apocalypse of St John*. Lecture-course, Nuremberg 1908 [GA 104], Lecture 9.

of both cosmic pillars[*] and the cosmic trees). In all this we do not only find the point of contact between Buddha and Christ but also the quite decisive point in which the life of Christ surpasses that of Buddha. The overcoming of death, the connection with and transformation of the Earth, resurrection, transubstantiation are, as we saw, these decisive points which show us the progress *from Buddha to Christ.*

And yet we would miss something most important if it were not emphasised that a meaningful divining of these things is already contained in the gospel of Buddha. That transformation of the earthly element that is portrayed at the altar in the transformation of bread and wine is still missing with Buddha. But the narration of Buddha's death contains a distant reminiscence of this at first where that strange last meal with the smith Chunda is narrated, after the eating of which Buddha is seized by the illness leading to his death. No one, it is said, would have been able to digest this meal in the right way, inwardly to transform it, except the perfected Buddha. That he then dies, he describes as a necessity for the Earth and universal salvation.

The echo with transubstantiation is yet clearer in the following scene with the water. Exhausted by his illness, Buddha sits by the path under a tree and asks his disciple Ananda to draw water for him out of a little stream nearby. 'I thirst, Ananda, give me something to drink.' Ananda objects that just now 500 loaded wagons had gone through and muddied the water. But a little further on a little stream flows pure and clear where he will draw water. Buddha repeats the first plea and Ananda his objection. He only obeys with the third plea of the Master, and behold, the water of the little rivulet suddenly flows pure and clear. 'Then the Holy One drank the water.'

With Buddha here the transformation of soiled into pure water, something impersonal, is spiritually meaningful. Only Christ takes the step towards the 'I', through which the personal element is laid hold of, and is led upwards again towards the purity of the impersonal while still retaining the ego-quality. He leads the transformation, which with Buddha remains within the impersonal quality of water, into that substance that can be for us a picture of the personal ego-nature, that is, into wine. Transformation of water into wine would consequently be the Christian continuation of the picture that we meet with Buddha as

[*] *Cf.* the two pillars in Solomon's Temple (1 Chron. 7: 21; 2 Chron. 3:17), and Rudolf Steiner, *Toward Imagination,* lecture 3, Berlin 20 June 1916 [*Weltwesen und Ichheit,* GA 169]. (The pillars of birth and of death, the transition from the spirit to the body, and from the body again to the spirit.)

merely a purification of water. If we then place next to this picture the other one in John's Gospel that tells of the miracle of the transformation of water into wine at the wedding in Cana, then through these two pictures we can look at that which for human consciousness signifies the step from Buddha to Christ.

Of decisive importance for the whole question 'from Buddha to Christ' is the section (Chapter 3) of the Mahāparinibbānasutta,* which precedes the passage already touched on above. It clearly shows that what is said here concerning the whole difference between Buddha and Christ lies in connection to the Earth, to death, resurrection and transubstantiation—Buddha disappears from the Earth into *nirvāṇa,* whereas the Christ unites Himself permanently with the Earth through the Mystery of Golgotha and takes part in earthly evolution. This does not involve some kind of merely modern occult theory, but in the spirit of the Buddha the whole question was already present. What becomes of earthly evolution only in Christ and through Christ, Buddha places as a possibility before his favourite disciple Ananda at a moment of his life that carries earthly destiny. Something similar to that which only 500 years later took place in the Mystery of Golgotha might have appeared already in Buddha's time, that a being advanced to a cosmic spirituality—in this case not the Christ-Sun-Being, but the Buddha inspired by Venus-Mercury—would have united with the Earth and its development till the end of earthly days. If Buddha's word had found a different resonance in the heart of him to whom it was directed, the whole of Earth evolution would have been different. Already in Buddha's era an event would have occurred which then could only happen at another point in time and in another spiritualised form.

It is not without significance that the Earth's being is considered in the whole section much more than is the case anywhere else with Buddha. Already at the beginning of the chapter, Buddha points to the beauty of the Earth in seeing the graceful cities that he especially loved and which he now views for the last time. This observation dedicated

---

* A translation of this beautiful Buddhist text, this decisively important text for the question of Buddha and Christ, appears in the volume *Buddha's Passing* (1925) (forthcoming). It offers the opportunity to follow the exact details of what is only indicated here. [See further on this important subject Prof. Beckh's major essay 'Buddha's Passing with excerpts from the Pali canon' in *From the World of the Mysteries,* and '*Nirvāṇa* and the Mystery of the Earth with Buddha: A Christian viewpoint on the future' from *Collected Essays and Articles* (forthcoming)—Tr. addition).]

to the earthly conditions reaches its climax with that strange teaching of Buddha about the eight causes of the earthquake, which is also in its musical, rhythmical relationship typical of Buddha's style of speaking. Also the essence of colour and its meaning for the meditative life is mentioned in this section.

Before his last parting from the town of Vesali, Buddha speaks to his favourite disciple Ananda:*

> Charming, O Ānanda, is Vaiśālī, charming are its sacred places; whoever, O Ānanda, allows the four elements of supernatural perfection (*iddhi*, Skt. *ṛddhi*) to become strong in himself can, if he wants to, prolong his life until the end of the era. The Tathāgata however, O Ānanda, rules and masters the four elements of supernatural power and has attained the highest perfection in this; he could, if he wanted to, prolong his physical existence until the end of the era.

(The elements are always listed as will, courage, the power of thinking, and the ability to fashion thinking pictorially.)

But Ananda does not understand the clear hint given to him; he misses the chance to ask Buddha to remain in existence, because, as the legend adds, Mara ensnared his heart. Then Buddha dismisses his disciple from his presence. Ananda places himself at some distance under a tree. (At the end of the chapter, we hear that all this did not happen for the first time, but that already on various occasions at various places Buddha had addressed the same words to Ananda without meeting understanding.)

After Ananda withdraws, the stage of events of the mystery-drama transfers itself from the physical to the supersensory world. Mara, the Buddhist Lucifer—a later chapter is devoted to this important Indian parallel to the Christian tempter—approaches Buddha, demanding that he enter into *nirvāṇa* since his earthly task is fulfilled (Mara-Lucifer, the champion of spiritual ecstasy that is removed from the Earth, is concerned to hinder the permanent union of Buddha's being with the Earth). On previous occasions Buddha had always counteracted Mara, which duty he still had to fulfil for all the disciples, and the lay brothers and sisters. They all had to become exact experts and true preservers of the teaching, and had to achieve full security in the

* Here Buddha alludes to what links Indian Yoga, as it were as forces of the Tree of Life, with the Tree of Knowledge. The Indian Buddhist word for these spiritual powers of the Holy One and his disciple is *iddhi* [Skt. *ṛddhi*] frequently mentioned in the text. *Cf.* H. B. *Buddha's Life and Teaching*, Germ. ed. Vol. 2, 72ff.

religious life. Only then would he be able to think of leaving the Earth and enter *nirvāṇa*. These concerns now no longer exist for Buddha; he answers Mara:

> Be unconcerned, you spiteful one, the Tathāgata's extinguishing will happen shortly; three months from today the Tathāgata will enter the great otherworldly *nirvāṇa*.

After the Buddha had given Mara this confirmation—here we stand, as with what follows, in the realm of occult events—he relieves himself (as mentioned above) of that inner pictorial power (*saṃskāra* or *sankhāra*), which builds the house of the physical body out of the etheric world and holds life fast in the body. Earthquakes and rolls of thunder accompany the event. The whole Earth, or the etheric body of the Earth, participates in that which is not only an inner soul-event of Buddha, but what at the same time is a cosmic event. (Precisely from the viewpoint of the question of Christ and the Earth all this is of highest interest; one can compare the earthquake with that of the death on Golgotha, and also the thunder with that of the Transfiguration: John 12:29.)

Terrified by the earthquake and the rolls of thunder, Ananda approaches and asks the Holy One the reason for the phenomena. Buddha gives him the already-mentioned eight reasons for the earthquake. The first reason lies more in the physical realm, in the relationship of the various earthly layers. With the second it has to do with the influences of specific spiritual and elemental beings. The six others touch on the inner sympathy with which the whole Earth, or rather the etheric Earth, participates in the great, world-moving experiences and events as the archetype of the life of a Buddha:

> When, O Ānanda, the Bodhisattva enters in wakeful consciousness into the earthly body of the mother, and when he in wakeful consciousness leaves the earthly body of the mother, then the forces of this Earth move, then it heaves and sways, trembles and shakes. When then the Perfected One awakens towards Buddha-enlightenment, and also, when he for the first time proclaims the teaching, then the forces of this Earth move, then it heaves and sways, trembles and shakes. When furthermore the Perfected One dismisses the working forces of his will for life and finally when he strips off all corporeality, disappears into the primordial ground of the world's breath (*nirvāṇa*), then the forces of the world move, then it heaves and sways, trembles and shakes.

Then Buddha admonishes Ananda for what he has missed, and tells of the promise he had now given to Mara. Then in Ananda there awakens the consciousness of what he had missed. His delayed plea to the Holy One to remain in existence comes now too late, and is rejected by Buddha.

> If you, Ānanda, (at the right time) had asked the Perfected One, then he would twice have denied you the request, but at the third time he would have fulfilled it for you. Therefore, Ānanda, you have done badly, therefore you have failed. Moreover, I have already clearly told you earlier: from all that we love, from everything dear to our heart, we have one day to separate ourselves, we have to let it go and say farewell to it. For, how would it be possible, Ānanda, that that which is born, has come about through the formative forces of existence and succumbs to the laws of decay, that this will not suffer decay? This would be something impossible. In the same way, the other matter is impossible, that the Perfected One would take back his will which he has relinquished and a word that he had spoken. This is something impossible.

And so Buddha lovingly seeks to comfort the disciple concerning what is unavoidable. Then he announces once more with certainty that in three months his *nirvāṇa*, his farewell from the Earth will follow.

Nowhere in Buddhist texts, and hardly anywhere in the whole history of the Earth, is the destiny of the Earth and the destiny of humanity placed onto the weighing scales in such a dramatically tense manner as here. Nowhere in the whole Indian literature do we stand in such a direct proximity to the great question of Christ and the Earth. Nowhere does the decisive significance of the expression 'from Buddha to Christ' come into view more clearly than here. Precisely here, where also the proximity to the Christian message is greatest, is shown most clearly how far distant we are with Buddha from the whole Christian resurrection, from everything that Christ has become for the Earth. And without somehow smudging all the significant differences of Christianity and Buddhism, nevertheless we can find how new depths of the Christian impulse can also arise for us here when we view this against the background of the events which took place half a millennium earlier on the soil of early India.*

* *Cf.* the whole section with the writer's essay from Buddhist Pali texts, 'Buddha's Relationship to Earthly Destiny. A most decisive moment in the life of the Buddha' [*Die Drei*, 1924. 4. Jg, Nr. 3. 57–65 & 181–92] Eng. tr. in *Collected Essays and Articles* (forthcoming).

III.

Knowledge: The Four Noble Truths and the Twelve Causes

The centre of Christianity is an event, a *deed;* the deed of life and death accomplished on Golgotha. The centre of Buddhism is a system of *knowledge.* Through the knowledge of enlightenment and the knowledge to become free from reincarnating the Bodhisattva became a Buddha. But the knowledge imparted to the world by Buddha was not to be merely accepted in faith. With the knowledge was combined the way along which the soul could approach the healing truth discovered by Buddha. Both knowledge and the way which leads to knowledge are comprised in the teaching of Buddha; the mere acceptance of a creed is far removed from it. This forms an important distinction between Buddhism and other religions, even that which passes in many circles for Christianity and the Christian confession of faith.

Through this the words '*from Buddha to Christ*' receive a new and earnest meaning. One thing is certain—in the matter of knowledge one does not remain with the Buddha of the past. But also the other fact is certain that Buddhist knowledge cannot be exchanged with a mere Christian belief, the mere believing acceptance of a Christian sectarian confession. Because many people today want knowledge instead of mere belief, this leads them to Buddha. On this path they miss Christ, or the possibility really to find Him. It is different when the soul inwardly proceeds *from Buddha to Christ.* The soul can no longer turn to a religious belief or feeling. But when the soul has inwardly taken up the impulse of Christ, it places the knowledge gained, or to be gained, into the light proceeding from the cross on Golgotha. In this light knowledge becomes life. The Tree of Knowledge becomes entwined with the Tree of Life. Through this life knowledge receives something like a metamorphosis, an inner transformation or revaluation. It is the essence of such a living knowledge that none of its levels is a closed, final stage, but each level of inner development knowledge too becomes something else. Such a living knowledge is nothing solid or rigid but an inner progressing, an eternal process of world-development and of human consciousness. The spiritual horizon it is not different from the physical one—every step forward creates it afresh. Thus the inner advance that took place for the Earth and humanity through Golgotha could also not without traces pass by the knowledge gained by Buddha under the sacred fig tree—the fig tree that Christ-Jesus passes withers and dies (Mark 11).

The knowledge gained by Buddha under the sacred fig tree is always represented in legend and doctrine as threefold. The first and second parts of this knowledge (the order varies) concern the destiny of beings in the cycle of rebirths, both on this side as well as the life between death and a new birth, that which is always called the knowledge of the great laws of destiny, or *karma,* and of reincarnation, of repeated earth-lives. The third part is the knowledge of *suffering,* its cause and its conquest. The well-known reflections on suffering contain the 'four noble truths', and the 'series of twelve causes'.

Belief in *karma,* the law of destiny, and in reincarnation is universal today in India, and already was so in the age of Buddha. But with Buddha—this is emphasised everywhere in the sacred tradition—it is not merely a matter of accepting a creed or dogma, but of a knowledge with direct vision that any disciple who followed the Path could make his own. As from a high watchtower one may see people walking in streets and squares, entering and leaving the houses, so it is said,* Buddha (and with him his disciples) saw in meditation, under the sacred fig tree, how beings—'men' are never directly mentioned—after the dissolution of the physical in death, take either the 'evil path' or the 'good path'. Because their actions are determined by their concepts, those who are led by a false world-view, by a lack of reverence, by evil thoughts, words and deeds, are set in dark places of torment. Those who are led by a right world-view, by reverence for the sublime, by good thoughts, words and deeds, reach the heavenly worlds of light, from which they return into earthly life. From *nirvāṇa,* however, accessible only to a Buddha, there is no return. Similarly, of the knowledge of repeated earth-lives it is said that under the fig tree Buddha had a perfectly clear recollection of his own earlier earth-lives, and that his disciples in meditation also recalled theirs to consciousness, though not with the same clarity as the Buddha himself. Those of all kinds who meditate, it is said, have their life-memories, but these are

* *Cf.* H. B. *Buddha's Life and Teaching*. Germ ed. II, 84, and I, 59.

dim as the glint of a glowworm, whereas with Buddha's disciples they are clear as the light of a lamp. With the elect they shine like the Morning Star. With the Buddha who has found enlightenment for himself alone, without imparting it to the world, they shine like moonlight, but with a world-redeeming Buddha, they are bright as the shining of a thousand suns.

The legend relates that when the Bodhisattva awoke from nocturnal meditation to Buddha-enlightenment in the first night-watch, with his super-sensory eyes he saw beings wandering, each according to his *karma*, through the light and dark regions on this side and the other; then, in the second night-watch, he turned his gaze to the vision of his own earlier earthly lives. With the super-sensory eye he saw these earthly lives and those of other beings through countless cosmic ages past, with all their vicissitudes of joy and sorrow, of high and lowly destinies. As he sees them, he remembers the name he bore in each of these incarnations; in each he remembers his gender, his caste, the circumstances and duration of his life. As he who wakes from sleep can recall the dreams of many nights, so Buddha, 'wakened' from the long sleep of human consciousness, recalls the dreams of many earthly nights. Only someone who, like Buddha, has stripped himself of everything personal in the present earthly life, sees the whole chain of incarnations, not only this one life that has now become strange to him.

The two branches of knowledge are very closely connected, that of *karma*, the law of destiny, and that of repeated earthly lives. For meditative knowledge finds that through the deeds of the one life, the destiny of the following incarnation is determined. This knowledge of *karma* and reincarnation is deeply and decisively significant for the whole development of human consciousness, for the whole future destiny of the Earth and humanity. Already before the soul gains the faculty to penetrate even into karmic contexts through developing its supersensory organs, this recognition modifies the whole balance and feeling for life, for everything that it morally presents and achieves in life. It depends whether the soul feels it is a plaything of external forces that determine without choice or justice its birth and conditions of life, or whether one feels oneself a member of a great cosmic scheme in which everything is rationally harmonised. In the latter case one can say to oneself that destiny does not only come to one from without. Ultimately the soul carries in itself that element which, in bringing about the outer circumstances of life, comes to effect in the whole configuration of its destiny. *Karma* is one of those truths of which one gains a living understanding through a new orientation of one's own life. And in the knowledge of repeated earthly lives the soul finds its necessary inner completion. The feeling of moral responsibility with which the soul confronts its earthly tasks acquires a more earnest and solemn significance. The disciples of Buddha were able to acquire the knowledge of *karma* and reincarnation as a genuine super-sensory fact, when in their meditative exercises they reached the control of *saṃskāra,* the formative forces of existence, in the depths of their own consciousness.

What becomes of such knowledge in the light of Christ? Could it ever happen that in the soul's progress from Buddha to Christ this knowledge would no longer be needed? This can never be claimed. At this point it is of special importance to differentiate what has been carried down through the Christian Gospels of the past from the living activity of Christ for the future of the Earth. The seed of life laid into the Earth at Golgotha is also the seed of a knowledge growing towards the future and creating itself ever afresh. All this lies in the deep mystery how, on the cross of Golgotha, the Tree of Knowledge and the Tree of Life entwine; they as it were cross over each other. The Tree of Knowledge, the tree of Death, becomes through this again a Tree of Life; the Tree of Life on a higher level becomes again the Tree of Knowledge, a knowledge that now includes life. 'I have much more to say to you, more than you can now bear' (John 16:12 NIV), Christ says at the farewell to His disciples.

The question whether the biblical Gospels contain indications of karma and rebirth can be posed. We do not want to enter the theological debate here. But it can be said that what Christ with his finger writes into the Earth before the woman taken in adultery (John 8:6, 8) is nothing other than that encompassing law of destiny that is conditioned through the whole connection of man with the Earth that the Indian calls *karma.* And there is the question posed by the disciples concerning the one born blind (John 9:2), 'Rabbi, who sinned, this man or his parents, that he was born blind?' Whatever answer Christ then gives, it would make no sense were not the repetition of earthly life presupposed. But it nevertheless remains with such veiled indications. In this, too, there must have been some meaning at that time at the beginning of the Christian era. Outwardly this truth was not mentioned. Through the fact that the present earthly life was regarded as the only one, the personality was to be matured and consolidated.* Buddha certainly speaks of repeated earthly lives, but that part in us which passes from life to life, the personal, individual 'I', still remains with him in a shadowy uncertainty. The Christian impulse had to enter first. Into that knowledge which was initially proclaimed by Buddha as lacking the 'I' the 'I' was to be added through the impulse of Christ. For this the ego-impulse itself had to be brought to a certain maturity in human consciousness. The knowledge of repeated earthly lives was later to flow in from the East approximately 2000 years later, mainly through the Buddha-impulse—but then in a more penetrated form than with Buddha himself—at that moment when it had become an inner necessity for the progressive further development of human consciousness also in the West. In such a development the spiritual leadership of Christ governs, inspiring humanity.

If the soul now places the knowledge as understood here of the laws of destiny and of repeated earthly lives given by Buddha into the light of Christ, it will be transformed and its value altered in many ways. In particular those truths, which in Buddha's sense meant something only for the individual soul, now especially begin to gain meaning for the Earth itself and its development. Christ does not write in vain into the Earth the all-governing laws of destiny and *karma*. Certainly, with this he expresses the truth also known to the Indian, that the account of human deeds is written as with an invisible quill-pen into the spiritual ether of the world. But through the fact that he writes that account especially into the Earth, into the Earth that is in the process of becoming His body, quite a new moment enters that is not yet contained in the Buddhist version of this knowledge in its Indian version.†

For the Indian, also for the Buddhist, *karma* is a personal matter only. He who has fathomed the lore of *karma* in the Indian sense, will not see it as his special task even to try and create a favourable *karma* for himself. For such a *karma*, like any other, in the course of time would also hold the soul fast in the cycle of rebirths, which the Indian wishes to eliminate. To the Indian, any *karma* represents a debt which he desires to pay off as speedily as possible, a burden of which he desires to rid himself as soon as possible. For the individual who has succeeded in getting quit of his individual debt to existence by the

* *Cf.* Rudolf Steiner, *The Gospel of St Luke/ According to Luke* [GA 114], lecture 10, and elsewhere.

† This teaching is also found in the Vedantic system, of Sankhya, Yoga, and elsewhere.

settlement of his karmic account, the further fate of the Earth and of humanity is without interest. This attitude which, from a higher point of view is undoubtedly an egoistic one, was justifiable in those last stages of man's descent. But it could not stand against the light in which, for the spiritual eye, the Earth again began to shine when the Christ, the Sun-Being, was united with it in the Mystery of Golgotha. The Earth became henceforth the body of the Christ, the destiny of the Earth and human destiny the immediate concern of the Christ.

Everything earthly has its origin in the light of the spiritual world. Through the Fall of man it became estranged from the primordial light and became subject to the powers of gravity that weave the illusion of matter. The Earth originates out of spiritual rays of the Sun. 'That it too one day may become a Sun',* that it becomes penetrated again by the rays of the primordial light, for this reason the exalted Sun-Being, Christ Himself, has taken on the burden and weight of the Earth, has gone right through death on the Earth and the darkness of the Earth.

But the destiny of the Earth could be fulfilled according to the mind of Christ only if each soul were united, in individual freedom, with the 'I'-impulse of Christ. This cannot be done if the soul tries to settle its *karma,* its own personal reckoning, in the Indo-Buddhist way, by considering only the significance for itself and its former deeds. The soul indwelt by Christ considers also the consequences which its deeds may have for the Earth as a whole; the soul becomes conscious of the burden laid upon the *karma* of the whole Earth by its individual *karma;* it feels its share of responsibility in the *karma* and future of the planet. Looking upon the Earth and humanity in this way, the soul also sees the Being who is united with the soul of the Earth, Christ, Who governs the future of the Earth and humanity. The soul sees that Christ has taken upon Himself what its deeds have brought upon the Earth, in order to restore it in the process of time to a balance, a harmony, so that all the discord of the Earth caused by human *karma* may, in future ages, be restored by Christ to a harmonious balance. And therein the soul sees the deep meaning of the Christian forgiveness of sin.

It is not that the individual soul is relieved of anything for which a higher feeling of responsibility makes it accountable. Had the Christian forgiveness of sins such a personal, egoistic meaning, there would be

* 'Daß auch sie einst Sonne werde', the final line of the poem 'Licht ist Liebe' by Christian Morgenstern in the collection *Wir fanden einen Pfad* (1914) ('We found a path'), dedicated to Rudolf Steiner. (online: http://www.gutenberg.org/ebooks/9623)—*Tr. note.*

no progress in it, it would be rather a retrograde step towards the Indo-Buddhist knowledge of *karma.* But when through anthroposophy Christian forgiveness is rightly understood in its depth* the knowledge of *karma* is embraced in its wide scope. Nothing is deducted from this knowledge as Buddha saw it under the sacred fig tree. But when the Buddhist knowledge is placed in the light shining from the cross of Calvary, there flows from it an impulse of will that is entirely new, and not that of the early Indian. In this new impulse Christ is the ruler. Under its influence, man will no longer desire only to free himself as rapidly as may be from the burden of his personal *karma.* He will consent to his destiny, taking it upon himself through the power of Christ. He can no longer desire that any part of his destiny should be personally remitted; it will be the wish of his heart to bring harmony into all that his deeds have done to the evolution of the Earth, not that he may be freed from the necessity of further incarnations, but that the human prototype darkened by sin may, in future ages rise again in ever more perfect and pristine purity. Man will bear his destiny throughout his incarnations in order to collaborate, in the light of Christ, with the restoration of the divine human type, to work willingly with Christ at the new Earth, to help in the building of the human future. And therein lies the true forgiveness of sins, that the soul—when it thus boldly takes upon itself its personal destiny and resolves to collaborate in building the temple of humanity—can be assured that through Christ it is relieved from the oppressive consciousness of having irreparably spoilt something in this temple-building by its past deeds. Just because the soul has courage to bear its destiny, to take the personal result of its deeds upon itself, a higher power is enabled to take on the objective significance of those deeds that extends beyond the personal, over the whole Earth. The Sun-power of Christ, which has now become the spirit of the Earth, can do this.

When the soul has united itself with the light of Christ, impulses unlike Buddha's that seeks to annihilate existence, but which are in the highest sense of the word creative of existence, flow from the knowledge of *karma.* This is the fundamental revaluation through Christ of

* Rudolf Steiner, *Christ and the Human Soul,* lecture 3 (Norrköping, 15 July 1914) [GA 155, 12–16 July 1914]. Here is differentiated the forgiveness of sins as a *cosmic* fact and forgiveness of sins as a *karmic* fact. It is emphasised that the saying, 'Your sins are forgiven you', means a *cosmic, not a karmic fact,* and that Paul's saying, 'Not I, but the Christ in me' has at the same time the earnest meaning, 'Not I and my self-redemption, but the Christ in me and the redemption of the Earth'.

Buddha's law of destiny (*karma*), which is of such deep significance for all mankind. The knowledge itself is not in any way changed by this revaluation, but what is laid hold of is the will-impulse flowing from it. Love towards one's destiny, acceptance of one's destiny, acceptance of the Christ-filled future of the Earth flows into the soul when it truly unites itself with the Christ-impulse.

*

All this already points to the revaluation that Indian Buddhist knowledge of repeated earthly lives receives through the Christ-impulse. The orientation of the Indian, especially the disciple of Buddha, towards this knowledge was always not to regard the repeated earthly life as a wished-for continuation of one's being, but as a continuation of suffering the ending of which was the most ardent wish to the Indian. Put into Christian terms, the Indian could only look at earthly existence and its repetition as a consequence of the Fall of man (in Indian terms: of the archetypal error, the human archetypal erring, *avidyā*). The aim of his spiritual, religious striving was to extinguish that error in himself, but with this also to dig out the root of earthly existence itself. Someone who penetrates into such depths in meditation as Buddha did under the sacred fig tree perceives in the depths of his consciousness the forces and stirrings of the will which fashion existence (as *saṃskāra*, or *sankhāra*).* Out of this inner vision there arose for him no other impulse of will than to give that strength which he had learnt to govern, the direction that it should not furthermore function: 'House-builder, you have been seen. Henceforth you will no longer build this house' (see above p. 7). That the formative forces, *sankhāra*, are not eternal, that they can be stopped—this was the great quintessence of all Buddha's knowledge. And the disappearance of the *sankhāras* was felt as the highest inexpressible bliss. *Nirvāṇa* (extinguishing), the aim of all Buddhist striving, was called the condition in which the *sankhāras* had been extinguished, the spiritual sphere where a return to earthly existence would no longer occur.

All this changed in the deepest sense on Golgotha. Here, too, the root

---

**Saṃskāra* is the Sanskrit form, *sankhāra* the Pali form of the word. Pali, the language of Buddhism today, relates to Sanskrit as Italian does to Latin. The Yogasūtra of Pātañjali is important to understand the concept *saṃskāra*. Especially with regard to this concept, specific lines of correspondence exist to the *Philosophie des Unbewussten* [1869] of Eduard v. Hartmann (1842–1906).

of the forces fashioning existence, the *sankhāras*, were deeply touched, deeper than ever before. Then the zero-point of human consciousness was reached, towards which humanity during Buddha's time was still moving. The forces of consciousness fashioning existence could be given directions towards confirming and creating the future.

For Christ Himself a repetition of the earthly, physical life did not come into question. He remained spiritually connected with the Earth—which had become His body—after He went through this physical earthly life and the physical earthly death. Yet, in order to connect ever more deeply in his soul with Christ and in this way creatively collaborate in the great task of the Earth of humanity, the human being needs repeated earthly lives. This gives him the opportunity to extinguish ever more in himself the consequences of the Fall and to become gradually similar to the great archetypal picture of the divine image of the human being.* From Buddha he may at least learn to release the personal connection to the urges of lower existence, but also, when this connection of the passions has been released, the soul has to wish, out of Christ, to give the forces fashioning existence the direction towards the repetition of earthly life. Because he knows that since the Mystery of Golgotha Christ is connected to the Earth, the human being no longer wishes to turn his back on the Earth prematurely, in order to disappear into some kind of *nirvāṇa*. But he knows that his own future destiny in the highest sense is connected with the destiny of the Earth. He remains with his conscious will with the Earth, because he feels he is a member of the great connection of cosmos and Earth. He has ceased working only at his personal redemption and instead collaborates with the redemption of the Earth.

Thus Christianity receives, on the one hand, a meaningful, deep enrichment through receiving the visionary knowledge of repeated earthly lives Buddha gained under the sacred fig tree. We see the Christ-impulse does not deny other great impulses of humanity, but is able to incorporate them. And, on the other hand, we see how out of

---

*Here it is important what Rudolf Steiner relates in the lecture-course *The Inner Nature of Man and Life between Death and Rebirth*, Vienna, 9–14 April 1914 [GA 153], lecture 2: something similar exists as an earthly-religious feeling looking up to the divine, for the divine world a kind of religion of the gods, which then in reverse manner looks to the human being, for the completion and gradual perfecting of the human image darkened through the Fall of man. The wish to flee from future earthly lives is in this sense nothing other than 'to become irreligious with regard to spirit-land'.

that knowledge—through the fact that it takes up the Christ-impulse into itself and is taken up by it—it becomes completely different, a will-impulse, completely different from the Buddhist one. With the knowledge of repeated earthly lives one sees most clearly what it means for the soul when it can inwardly take the step from Buddha to Christ.

*

In what has been presented here is also included the inner revaluation of that Buddhist knowledge usually presented as the central one,* the revaluation of the realisation of suffering, its cause and its overcoming. The Earth ceases to be a mere place of suffering for someone who knows and feels that Christ has connected Himself to the Earth. What is said about that Buddhist 'truth of suffering' (the third of the Three Great Truths gained by Buddha under the fig tree) and its revaluation in the light of the Christ-impulse, we cannot express more poignantly and in a finer manner than in those words taken from an Easter lecture by Rudolf Steiner (Cologne, 11 April 1909. GA 109):

> The Buddha had seen a corpse and had recognised from it the nothingness of life. Men who lived six hundred years after the Event of Golgotha looked up with fervent devotion to the corpse on the cross. For them it was the token of life, and in their souls dawned the certainty that existence is not suffering, but leads beyond death into blessedness. Six hundred years after the Event of Golgotha the corpse of Christ-Jesus on the cross became the token of life, of the resurrection of life, the overcoming of death and of all suffering, just as six hundred years before the Mystery of Golgotha the corpse was the sign that suffering must be the lot

* For greater clarification, the words of the famous Buddhist passage on suffering (*cf.* H. B. *Buddha,* Vol. 1, 67) from the 'Sermon of Benares' should once more be quoted here. The whole quote from Steiner in the text also refers to this.
'These, my disciples, are the four noble truths of suffering, of the origin of suffering, of the annihilation of suffering, of the path which leads to the annihilation of suffering: birth is suffering, old age is suffering, illness is suffering, death is suffering, to be united with what one does not love or separated from loved ones is suffering, not obtaining one's wishes is suffering—in short, the five ways of grasping the sensual are suffering. The origin of suffering is sensual desire (*tṛṣṇā,* 'thirst'), which leads to rebirth, is accompanied by passion and which lusts here and there. Overcoming suffering is the annihilation of sensual desire, the perfect freedom from passion. The path which leads to overcoming suffering is the noble eightfold path: right vision, right thoughts (decision), right speech, right action, right living, right effort, right awareness, right meditation.'

of man driven into the physical world by the thirst for existence. Never was there a greater reversal in the whole course of human evolution.

If, six hundred years before our era, entrance into the physical augured suffering for man, how does the great truth that life is suffering present itself to the soul after the Mystery of Golgotha? How does it present itself to men who look with understanding at the cross on Golgotha? Is birth, as the Buddha declared, suffering? Those who look with understanding at the cross on Golgotha, and feel united with it, will gladly tread this Earth upon which Christ has walked. Union with Christ kindles in the soul the power to find its way up into the spiritual worlds, bringing the realisation that birth is not suffering but the portal to the finding of the Redeemer, Who clothed Himself with the very same earthly substances which compose the bodily sheaths of human beings.

Is illness suffering? No! Even if humanity today cannot yet understand what the spiritual life is in truth that streams from the Christ, in the future they will learn to understand it. They will know that one who lets himself be permeated by the Christ-impulse can overcome all illness through the strong healing forces he unfolds from within himself. For Christ is the great Healer of mankind. His power embraces that with which illness can be overcome. Illness is not suffering. Illness is an opportunity to overcome an obstacle through the strength of the Christ-power developed in the human being.

Mankind must arrive at a similar understanding about the infirmities of old age. Age is not suffering, for with every day that passes we grow into the spiritual world. So too, death is not suffering, for death has been conquered through the Event of Golgotha.

Can separation from what we love still be suffering? No! Souls permeated with the Christ-power know that love can forge links from soul to soul that cannot be severed. There is nothing between birth and death and between death and a new birth to which we cannot find the way through the Christ-impulse. The Christ leads us to union with what we love.

Equally, to be united with what we do not love cannot be suffering, because the Christ-impulse teaches us to love all things in their due measure. The Christ-impulse shows us the way and in finding it there can no longer be suffering, for there is nothing that we do not encompass with love. So, too, not to attain that for which we yearn can no longer be suffering, for longings are so purified and ennobled through the Christ-impulse that people yearn only for what they should. They no longer suffer from what they are compelled to renounce; for if they must renounce anything, it is for the sake of purification, and the Christ-power enables them to feel it as such. Consequently, renunciation is no longer suffering.

What, in essence, does the Event of Golgotha signify? It signifies the

> gradual elimination of the facts associated with suffering by the great Buddha.

Thus far, a passage from Rudolf Steiner in which—here as elsewhere—it is said that Buddha spoke correctly. 'Why could Christ work effectively?' he asks,* and answers, 'Because Buddha spoke the truth.' Buddha spoke correctly of the great facts of the world's suffering out of the conditions of his age, but these facts themselves are overcome on the cross of Golgotha; they are overcome for everyone to the measure that one knows how to unite inwardly with the Impulse raying from the cross.

We find conceivably the most complete overcoming of Buddha's viewpoint with Novalis, the great forerunner of a spiritually penetrated, esoteric Christianity. Out of a deep feeling of the Christ-impulse Novalis speaks in his Fragments of 'enthusiasm for illnesses and pain', of death as the closer connection of loving beings. 'Every illness,' he says, 'is perhaps a necessary beginning of more intimate union of two beings, the necessary beginning of love ... Does not everywhere the best [thing] begin with illness?' In a meaning touching on Buddha's recognition of suffering in the world, but at the same time completely changing this knowledge, Novalis recognises the deep connection of life with that which is pain and illness, of death with that which is the innermost essence of health, that which is the hidden strength of healing:

> *Im Tode ward das ewige Leben kund,*
> *Du bist der Tod, und machst uns erst gesund!*
> In everlasting life death found its goal,
> For thou art Death who at last mak'st us whole.†

It has to be emphasised once more that this assessment of suffering, this other relationship to illness and death, is realised for the soul to the extent that it has found in the heart the connection with the Christ. For the soul that has not found Christ remains with the 'truth of suffering' presented by Buddha:

> Birth is suffering, old age is suffering, illness is suffering, death is suffering, to be united with what one does not love or separated from loved ones is suffering, not obtaining one's wishes is suffering.

---

* Rudolf Steiner, *The Spiritual Hierarchies and their Reflection in the Physical World.* Lecture, Düsseldorf, 12 Jan., am. 1909 [GA 110].

† From *Hymns to the Night*, tr. George MacDonald.

The Twelve Causes

The version just outlined is not the only one that Buddha gave of his great realisation. But where he found it under the sacred fig tree, where its inner construction gradually appeared before his spiritual vision, it initially stood before him as that well-known series of 'twelve causes' (see *Buddha*, I, 60f. II, 94ff.).* Approaching the explanation of this scheme in the light raying from the Christian impulse, we then find that precisely in its deep value for knowledge, indeed in its true, higher meaning, this scheme (which at all times was very difficult to explain) it is really only understandable in this Christian light.† In it we can find how this scheme—one would like to say, with an astonishing degree of occult-scientific geniality—develops that which, in Christian terms, presents the results of the Luciferic influence in the Fall of man through all the levels of consciousness, right through the inner nature of man. The scheme presents a kind of story of the creation of human consciousness and existence, but precisely a story of that creation that took place through the agency of Lucifer in earthly evolution. The Bible, if we look carefully, speaks of a threefold creation (*cf.* H. B. *Our Origin in the Light*):

---

*Here again for clarity the 12 stages of the series (the structure is as follows: '2 arises through inward connection with 1, 3 arises through inward connection to 2', and so on until the 12th. Likewise the reverse: 'Through overcoming 1, 2 is overcome, through overcoming 2 then 3' and so on):

1. *avijjā* (Skr. *avidyā*) ignorance, error;
2. *sankhāro* (*saṃskāra*) power forming existence, formative forces (*cf.* Schopenhauer's 'will');
3. *viññāna* (*vijñāna*) sentient consciousness;
4. *nāma-rūpa*, name and form;
5. *saḷāyatana* (*ṣaḍāyatana*) the six senses;
6. *phasso* (*sparṣa*) touch;
7. *vedanā*, the feelings;
8. *taṇhā* (*tṛṣṇā*) thirsting desire;
9. *upādāna*, laying hold of sensory existence;
10. *bhava*, becoming in sensory existence (pregnancy);
11. *jāti*, birth;
12. *jarā – maraṇa – soka – parideva – dukkha – domanassa – upāyāsā*, old age, death, sorrow, lamentation, suffering, sadness and despair.

†It is already presented in this light by Rudolf Steiner in *The Gospel of St Luke/According to Luke* [GA 114], lecture 3.

1. the creation through the Elohim of the archetypal, spiritual human being (Gen. 1:27);
2. the creation through Yahveh of the—still supersensible—earthly human being (Gen. 2:7);
3. the creation of the physically dense, earthly human being, the placing of the human being in the dense earthly element, through Lucifer and Ahriman (Gen. 3–11).

The Mystery of the first and second of these three creations is as if lost in Buddhism, even if Buddha himself knew of it—he did not reveal to the world everything that he knew.* In any case, it does not form part of his teaching. For only through the Christ, through Golgotha has it become possible to find again that which has become lost in the human make-up, the lost divine image of the human being, and thereby also the Mystery of the divine creation of the human being. It is consequently fully justified in historical development that Buddha tells us only the mystery of the third of the three creations of the human being, the Mystery of the creation through Lucifer and Ahriman. This creation led the human being through the original sin of 'not knowing', of 'sensory desires', to a birth into dense matter, involving old age, death and suffering. This Mystery of the third creation, however, the effect of the Luciferic influence in man's being that finally subjects him to the (Ahrimanic) powers of death (Gen. 3:19), is presented in this Buddhist scheme with the greatest scientific geniality.

The error into which paradisal man fell through the temptation of Lucifer is, consequently, the first cause of these Buddhist twelve causes. By looking within, Buddha intends to tell us, the human being can discover this error, and from it all the others. That which he still has in his consciousness and that finally places him in this physical world of suffering and of death stands connected to this error. The first sentence correspondingly runs: 'Out of the error of not knowing (*avidyā*), there arises *sankhāra* (*saṃskāra*), the forces fashioning existence.' For Buddha this concerns the formative forces of the human ether-body into which the Luciferic influences have penetrated. The passionate Luciferic thirst for existence operates into the impulses and actions of the subconscious will, with everything that works on from life to life as the results of *karma*, governing rebirth, that is, with what the human being has become since the Fall of man. Buddha sees only these Luciferically tinged formative forces (what Schopenhauer calls the

* On this important point, see H.B. *Buddha*, Germ. ed. I, 115ff.

'will'); he deals only with these. For this reason he obliterates them, wipes them out root and branch, after becoming aware of their tendency. (For the Christ at this juncture there arises the pure power of existence, free from the Luciferic influence, purifying and spiritualising the earthly element that has become sinful, rebuilding the decayed 'house'.) Buddha calls this *sankhāra* the 'house-builder' whom he saw; he is no longer to build the house of physical existence. (We find him again in the 'Ferryman' of Goethe's *Fairytale,* and in the 'Spirit of the Elements' of Steiner's *Mystery Dramas.*)

From *sankhāra,* the sleeping subconscious, the creation Buddha refers to proceeds to *viññāna,* the sentient consciousness, to what in anthroposophy is called the astral element. The Luciferically tinged formative forces influence the Luciferically tinged consciousness. In three stages from the physical to the astral, the becoming human being is here built up for us—for here, too, *avijjā,* 'not knowing', seen in outer nature corresponds to the deep unconscious condition of the physical, mineral element.

The fourth stage enters that of the 'I'. Here too the Luciferic influence enters. Through it the true higher human 'I' becomes lost. What remains is the semblance and mere shadow of personality, or as Buddha calls it 'name and form', *nāma-rūpa.* Out of consciousness, name and form arise, the appearance and shadow of personality, the false ego-consciousness. We recognise the Buddhist teaching of the 'non-ego'—overcome through Christ and Golgotha—puts 'name and form' in place of the true 'I'. In the nature of the case, this is deeply founded in the whole configuration of the consciousness of humanity at that time. It rightly expresses what has entered the creation of man through Lucifer.

The subjective element of the lower, false ego affects the senses. 'Out of name and form (*nāmarūpa*) the six senses (*ṣaḍāyatana*) arise', Buddha says, speaking of the fifth cause. The senses now arise as they have become through Lucifer, as that which ensnares the human being in the sensory realm, where he succumbs to the forces of death.

The downward trend is continued, clearly shown in the subsequent stages. The senses lead through the sense of touch, *phasso* (*sparśa*), to *vedanā,* sensation in general, which is now thoroughly corrupted by the Luciferic error (*avidyā*) that formed the beginning of the series. Out of this contact the thirsting of sensuous desire, *taṇhā* or *tṛṣṇa,* follows that leads on to the seizing of the desired object, *upādāna,* or as we could say, the biblical 'biting of the apple'.

We have now reached the ninth stage. The next stage is the actual Fall of man, the transference into a physical body, *bhava*. This leads, in the eleventh stage through conception to birth, *jāti*, and birth leads into physical life that brings suffering, age and death, *jarā, maraṇa, soka-parideva, dukkha* and *domanassa-upāyāsā*. If in the place of Buddha's chosen abstractions we were to name the essential cause, then at the point of departure, of the original sin of 'not knowing', in the primordial error, it is Lucifer; in the concluding stage of old age, death and suffering, it is Ahriman. The series comes about, inwardly consistent, from Lucifer to Ahriman; from sensory desire, the original sin of the first human couple leads into the realm where the human being succumbs to the weight of the earthly element, the powers of death.

*

In all this we only see what Lucifer has made of the human being, not what he can become through Christ. Buddha wanted to reverse all that Lucifer had brought about. For this reason he follows the series of causes with a developmental series by which the downward development might be undone. Out of mastering error there follows the mastering of the formative forces as far as the overcoming of old age, death and suffering. However, as always emphasised here, mastering in such a way that rebirth is eliminated, and with this the inevitable repetition of death also disappears. In Buddha's teaching death itself is not really overcome; it is not converted into life. The problematic series of causes that has led the human being from the original error into death and suffering of physical existence is only unrolled in reverse order. The forward movement in creation in the sense of the advance of divine being is thereby not achieved. Only the Christ-impulse gives the formative forces of existence the new, creative direction; it alone is able to lead to regain the lost divine archetype of the human being; it alone leads, beyond Lucifer's creation, once again into the kingdom of creative becoming in the sense of the progressive divine powers of cosmic evolution. And so the profound recognition of the Buddhist series of causes is fully justified in the light of Christ, and yet in its negative results overcome by a new positivity.

The light of the Christ-impulse also overcomes that which we feel as a dead abstraction in Buddha's conceptual formulations. Buddha himself took the step to images by speaking of the *saṃskāras* as 'house-builder'. The later Tibetan Mahayana Buddhism went further in this direction. We see everywhere that consciousness becomes pictorial again in this phase of Buddhism (see p. 13f. above) falling in the Christian era. The conceptual series that was gradually felt as too abstract is raised in this area of Mahayana Buddhism into a pictorial representation. In Tibet:

- *avidyā*, error, primordial sin, is presented as a blind woman,
- *saṃskāra*, the formative force, as a porter,
- *vijñāna*, that (astral) consciousness human beings share with the animal world, as a monkey,
- *nāmarūpa*, the personality, as a ship crossing the ocean,
- *ṣaḍāyatana*, the senses, as a house (house of the physical body), and also as eyes peering through a mask,
- *sparśa*, touch, as a kiss of a loving couple,
- *vedanā*, the feelings, as an arrow hitting the eye. Furthermore,
- *tṛṣṇa*, thirsting longing, was represented as a thirsty person drinking eagerly,
- *upādāna*, the Buddhist 'bite into the apple', by the plucking of fruit from a tree.

The remaining stages appeared as:

- a pregnant woman,
- a woman in labour, and finally
- an old man, or also a corpse being carried to burial.

The similarity of one image with one in the Bible [taking the apple] is worth noticing.

Mahayana Buddhism arrives at this picturing of the abstract Buddhist sequence of concepts. Christ brings us not only to the consciousness of pictures, but through the pictures into the living intuition of real cosmic forces at work. Someone today, as people already did in the later period of ancient India, forms abstract concepts, observing in his concepts and imaginations the world and his own being. The more he develops this stage, the more the human being arrives at the point of regarding the world and its events no longer from the personal viewpoint. The cosmic perspective opens to his spiritual view; even in everything within and around him, he perceives the creative governing of the hierarchies. Something like the Buddhist series of causes no longer remains in its abstract, conceptual formulation. The gaze of the spiritual eye awakened through Christ penetrates through abstract concepts to the governing cosmic beings. The view no longer remains with what initially is only caused by Lucifer, but it penetrates through this 'third creation' into the mysteries of the primordial creation. Like a mirror-picture of these mysteries of the primordial creation, it then recognises the Buddhist series of causes.

- Behind *avidyā* it perceives the reigning of those powers that have implanted the primordial seed of physical existence—as that which sleeps in the deepest subconsciousness—into the development of the human being. Christian esotericism calls them the 'Thrones'.
- Behind *saṃskāra,* the formative forces working in the etheric world, it perceives the 'Spirits of Wisdom' (Kyriotetes), who weave the archetypal picture of the living etheric into the human being.
- Behind *vijñāna,* consciousness, it perceives the 'Spirits of Movement' (Dynameis) who inlay the astral element into the human being.
- Behind *nāmarūpa,* name and form, it perceives the 'Spirits of Personality' (Archai) and preceding them, the 'Spirits of Form' (Exusiai), who impregnate the 'I' into the human being, *etc.,* until in *vedanā,* the human being himself is reached, and following this with *tṛṣṇa,* sensual passion, the development subsides into the sub-human, elemental region.

All the tremendous pictures of cosmic development, as Rudolf Steiner directly perceived them in his book *Esoteric/ Occult Science, an Outline,* also arise in this order of Buddhist concepts when we allow the light of the Christ-impulse to illuminate them. We see through them to the Twelvehood of zodiacal powers; the Buddhist Twelve Causes itself mirrors the number twelve. It is the great Twelvehood of the heavenly signs through which the Christ in the primordial beginning of the world has creatively poured out his Being, that Twelvehood that attains a deeper cosmic symbolism in the group of Twelve disciples gathered around Him, the Thirteenth. In this way the soul, by inwardly taking the creative step from Buddha to Christ, is led out of the still abstract element of Buddha's knowledge into the living depths of Christian knowledge.

IV.

The Way

East, West and the 'I'

The Buddha's knowledge has its main support through the Way that leads to it, through the Path. When Buddha first revealed to the world the truth which dawned upon him under the Bodhi tree during the sacred night of his enlightenment, when he 'set the wheel of learning rolling over the Earth', as the pictorial descriptions of the traditions put it, the first thing he proclaimed was the Path, the 'excellent eightfold middle Way'.* The second thing is the fourfold statement concerning suffering, the coming into existence and the relief from suffering; in the fourth part the Path reappears as the 'Way that leads to the extinguishing of suffering'. Buddha's teaching of the Eightfold Path is not exhausted in the short formula:

right understanding,
right resolution/ decision,
right speech/ word,

---

* 'Two paths, my disciples, are to be avoided by one who has entered the spiritual life: the path of the satisfaction of sensual desire (*kāma*) which is low, mean, unworthy of the noble and pointless, which does not lead to holy life, to renunciation, to freedom from passion, to realisation, to awakening, to *nirvāṇa*; and the path of self-torture which is painful and pointless, and which is followed by suffering in this visible as well as in the future life. Avoiding these two directions, the Tathāgata is proclaiming the norm of the middle path which is right vision, right thought, right speech, right action, right living, right effort, right awareness, right meditation. Avoiding these two extremes, you disciples, the Perfected One has discovered the *Path of the Middle*, which opens up the spiritual eye, revealing understanding, which leads to peace of mind, to vision, to enlightenment, to *nirvāṇa*. It is the noble Eightfold Path, which is: right understanding, right resolution, right speech, right deed, right livelihood, right endeavour, right mindfulness, right meditation. This, you disciples, is the Path of the Middle, discovered by the Perfected One, which opens the spiritual eye, revealing knowledge, which leads to peace of mind, to vision, to enlightenment, to *nirvāṇa*' [from the Sermon of Benares].

right action/ deed,
right livelihood/ conduct,
right endeavour,
right mindfulness,
right meditation.

Another more detailed instruction about the path of inner development is given in many of Buddha's discourses. It consists of four stages, advancing from the first, preparatory stage of moral purification to meditation, through meditation to knowledge, and through knowledge to inner emancipation. In its richness, this teaching first points towards the actual Mystery of the path, as it had already lived in the earlier Mystery-wisdom, in India already before Buddha in the teaching of Yoga. From the mere outer communication and acceptance of the knowledge in a still more abstract language, the path leads to its real inner experience through a realm of pictures and of sounding rhythms. In the whole presentation that pictorial element is living there. These sounding rhythms, so characteristic of Buddha's entire teaching, can tell us more today than the abstract content of the teaching itself. We can feel the pictorial world in the description of the 'Path' like a shadow in all that was present in the Yoga initiation. Already through the fact that Buddha uses the word 'Way', or 'Path', for development taking place completely in the spiritual realm, he speaks to us in a meaningful picture.

The real greatness and permanency of what Buddha has bequeathed to the world lies in the teaching of this Path. Not that all the details of it are valid for all time. The Path, as it can be communicated to any particular age by the great teachers of humanity, is yet only a fraction of that which is seen or divined as 'the Path' in the light of eternity. Here too then, the step from Buddha to Christ involves a renewal of method as well as of goal. The greatness of Buddha's message lies in the fact that the Path, up to his time kept as a secret in Indian Yoga, known and practised only by exclusive communities, was now presented by Buddha to the world in a morally purified form and free from all sectarianism. Buddha's teaching is rightly spoken of as one of the great world-religions, for it does not depend on mere dogma, but is built upon a Path of Knowledge.

For Christian evolution in the West, the Path in itself is nothing new. There, too, Mystery traditions, communities and orders existed, in which sections of the Path could be found in a form adapted to the age. The Christian Gospels themselves and still more the Apocalypse contain, in profound pictures, secrets of the path of initiation, although in the popular Christian churches these things have been treated as though non-existent. In organised Christianity until very recently, creed and dogma reigned supreme. Only in poems, in myths and fairytales,* and in mystical writing have veiled allusions to the Christian path found their way into wider groups—for instance in the Quest of the Grail. Above all in this direction Wolfram's *Parzifal* from the thirteenth century was significant, similar in the French of Chrétien de Troyes. In the picture of the Holy Grail and the search for the Grail it points towards the mysteries of Christian initiation and to the path into the spiritual worlds, which was significantly to gain in importance in the future. Yet what is indicated there would have always remained a secret had not from another side a knowledge of the path flowed into the development. In Western spiritual life a clear path into higher worlds could not be found.

However, during the last quarter of the nineteenth century, with the growing recognition of supersensory facts, ever increasing groups felt the need to substitute for faith a knowledge of the spiritual worlds. People looked towards the East, to receive from there the light which the West seemed unable to offer. The way into the spiritual worlds was sought, and people found it, or thought to find it, in the Indian systems of Vedanta, Yoga or Buddhism. What attracted so many at that period to Buddhist and other Indian teachings was not so much its content—for that was too negative for Western minds—but rather the presence within it of the Way. This explains the influence which Neo-Buddhism, especially as presented in Mme. Blavatsky's theosophy, has exercised on Western spiritual life.†

In this manner much was brought over from the descending era of man's consciousness and established in the ascending era. In seeking the Indian spiritual paths, people lost the Christ, the true guide to the 'I'. The formal Christianity of the churches and of the creeds closed themselves against the path. The Indo-Buddhist path, denying the existence of a real 'I', eliminates the Christ. How is the way from Buddha to Christ to be

---

* Concerning an appearance of the Christian path in the fairytale of 'Snow-white' [in the Grimms' collection], see *Die Christengemeinschaft*, 1. Jrg., 5. 138–46; Eng. tr. in Hermann Beckh, *Collected Essays and Articles* (forthcoming), also included in H. B. *Our Origin in the Light: Pictures from Genesis* (forthcoming).

† In particular Olcott and Sinnett connected to this stream of Buddha, whereas others referred to Brahmanism.

found? How can He who says to Himself: 'I am the way, the truth and the life' become once more a way for us into the spiritual worlds?

An epoch-making answer to this question was given at the beginning of the twentieth century in a book that is decisive for the process of human consciousness, Rudolf Steiner's *Knowledge of the Higher Worlds: How is it attained?* [GA 10]. Although the word 'Christ' is never once mentioned in the text,* its subject throughout is how we can find Christ on the path to the spiritual worlds. The second half of this book shows us how important the stages of the 'Eightfold Path' are for the development of the higher sense-organs† adapted to cosmic thinking, and how their content, left by Buddha as somewhat sketchy and undefined, today acquires a living meaning. The way of Buddha is recognised in a way as a fragment of the true Path, as it can be followed in a contemporary form in the present era.

For if today, in the light and with the guidance of Christ, we once more seek the way into higher worlds, this way is no longer as with Buddha a path upon which we turn our backs on a dying Earth-existence, but a path whereon we may collaborate with Christ in the renewal of that dying earth-existence. That this path, in spite of any points of contact with Buddha's path and with all the Mystery-paths that have ever been, is yet in every detail something intrinsically different has been shown by Rudolf Steiner in *Knowledge of the Higher Worlds: How is it attained?*‡ The Buddhist path and the Buddhist meditation can be fully practised only in cloistered retirement on the Earth, and yet already withdrawn from the Earth. At the same time it must be remembered that the spiritual atmosphere of India was still such that the effects of even a most exclusive spiritual effort were in a measure shared by others. The Indian felt, and still feels today, that the spiritual radiation of meditation extends in a wide sphere, protecting and blessing all created things. Yet in order to be a disciple of Buddha it was necessary to be separated from life to some degree, whereas every

---

*True, though the name, or rather title, does appear in a footnote mentioning a book-title by Thomas à Kempis, *De Imitatione Christi*—Tr. note.

†What is called the '16-petalled lotus-flower' (in Indian Yoga: *viśuddha*).

‡The path to the spiritual worlds is presented from various viewpoints in the final chapters of the book *Theosophy* [GA 9] and *Esoteric/ Occult Science: An Outline* [GA 13]; *A Way to Self-Knowledge* [GA 16]; *The Threshold to the Spiritual World* [GA 17]; and in addition numerous individual lectures and lecture-cycles. *Knowledge of the Higher Worlds* [GA 10] most directly takes into account the viewpoints and needs of practical life.

sentence of *Knowledge of the Higher Worlds* shows us that by following the Christian path in the spirit of Christ we do not separate ourselves from life but rather for the first time enter fully into life, learning by it to feel ourselves as parts of one great scheme of life. Everyday existence with all the tasks it brings us, far from being a hindrance to the spiritual life and to the practice of meditation, becomes the very opportunity and means whereby we train ourselves for the higher life. The Tree of the higher Knowledge is no longer separated from the Tree of Life. A spiritual life that is able in this way to permeate the earthly element, to absorb and transform it, must possess stronger forces than a spiritual life that, as Buddha sees it, merely hovers above the earthly element. And the stronger force that helps us also to permeate and transform the earthly element is none other than that of Christ. In Buddha's time, separation from the earthly element was still spiritually enjoined. Before Golgotha, spiritual life had no power to quicken and invigorate the dying earth-existence.

As we follow the path in the new Christian sense into the spiritual worlds, Christ's words 'I am the way' are laid open to us in their whole cosmic profundity, their cosmic power and cosmic weight. The path, which through all the early mysteries has led into the spiritual worlds, is absorbed by Christ into Himself. He fills the path with His essential Being, with His cosmic purposes, with His purposes for the Earth and humanity. And, above all, we must look at the first two words of the sentence, 'I am the way'. In the 'I-am' lies the secret of the new element which, through Christ, has entered into the way. This great 'I-AM' which is never extinguished, carries the consciousness through darkness and death, and becomes our Way, our Guide, our Light upon the path.

It is just this great I-am that is lacking in Buddha's path. Buddha's path does not lead, as Christ leads, to the finding of the 'I'. Buddha himself speaks quite clearly on this subject.[*] In meditation he, and with him his disciples, discover that the ordinary 'I' of the sense-world is initially not the true 'I'. Buddha realises, which [one 'I']—two such 'I's' or selves are mentioned—in the further progress of meditation is seen as a higher 'I' in the etheric and astral spheres.[†] At each further stage an illusory 'I' of the stage below is found to be nothing, a non-'I'. Buddhist

[*] *Cf.* H. B. *Buddha*. Germ. ed. II, 71f.

[†] The Buddhist *skandha* teaching counts five members of the human constitution; none of them is the 'I'.

meditation does not penetrate to the true, eternal 'I'. Buddha especially warns his disciple to turn away from all that is not eternal.

The eternal, the great star-harmonies of the cosmos, dwell in the consciousness of the Buddha. He sees mankind as severed from this harmony by the Fall into sin. The world is suffering as the result of error. Buddha sees man defiled by earthly existence. By cleansing him from this defilement, he desires to raise him, return him to the harmony of the star-spheres. This is only possible through the complete extinction of the false and turbid glamour of the earthly 'I'. (*Nirvāṇa* means extinction.) Buddha desired to extinguish the whole Luciferic creation of the earthly 'I'. Buddha could not speak of that which in the star-harmonies of the cosmos itself lives as the true 'I' of the human being, because this 'I' lost through the Fall of man is first only present through Christ.

We saw at the beginning that with the 'I' there the actual archetypal picture of the human being, the image of the gods (Gen. 1:27), is missing with Buddha. The path of Buddha only wants to extinguish the picture of the human being as it has become today through the Fall. The way of Christ is different. It is a way of new creation and resurrection. What above all must rise again is the human being himself, the lost prototype of man, the image of God, and with him and in him the human being's true higher 'I'. To this resurrection the Christian path aspires when pursued in earnest, as described in *Knowledge of the Higher Worlds*. On this path we learn that it is man whom we must find again. And we cannot find him until we have clearly seen the image of man sullied by his Fall, until we have realised all that our *karma*, the thoughts, feelings and deeds of former lives, has made of us. Organs of higher vision* are developed on the Christian path as well as on the

* Indians call them 'lotus flowers'; in his book *Knowledge of the Higher Worlds* Rudolf Steiner takes over the term. The Indian words for these organs are:
svādhiṣṭhāna (4-petalled);
maṇipūra (10-petalled);
anāhata (the 12-petalled lotus-flower in the heart);
viśuddha (16-petalled);
ājñā (2-petalled lotus-flower, between the eyes).
Moreover, on the Indian path—which, different from the Christian path, seeks the exit out of the round of rebirths:
sahasrāra, what is called the 1000-petalled lotus-flower on the crown of the head, through which the redeemed one in the moment of death leaves the body, in order no longer to return into earthly existence.

Buddhist path. But when Christ is the guide, the first picture presented in higher vision is that of our own nature, as it has become since the Fall, through the course of incarnations. A sullied image initially confronts us as a warning and a reproach, a phantom guardian. This Lesser Guardian keeps watch at the threshold of the spiritual worlds to protect the entrance into those worlds until we have effaced every stain in our character, and have consciously set our hands to the work of restoring the lost human image. Then it shows us our task for many earthly lives to come.[*] Not until we have learned to bear the sight of our past do we become spiritually ripe enough to receive the sight of the future in the figure of sublime light who stands as the second, the Greater Guardian, before the threshold of the spiritual worlds.

Then we understand that the path which has led us up to the spiritual worlds is the same as that which man followed in the reverse direction in his descent from the heights of his origin in the light to the darkness of the Earth.[†] The ascent into the higher worlds passes by the Guardian of the Threshold of Paradise who once drove man out into the sensory world.[‡] Only the valiant soul that is spiritually ready for this ascent and strong enough to endure the visionary sight of his own past is able to pass that Guardian. Behind him, the soul sees the figure of Christ, the soul's own divine prototype and higher 'I'.

This is described in *Knowledge of the Higher Worlds* as the meeting with the two Guardians of the Threshold. In this meeting, the human being finds his true, his eternal 'I'. Consequently, the Buddhist path that does not lead to the finding of the 'I', also has no knowledge of a 'Guardian of the Threshold'. Here we stand at the parting of the roads, where the Christian path differs from the Indian path of Buddha. When the disciple has found his higher 'I' in Christ, beyond the Greater Guardian, the crossing of the threshold and the entry into the spiritual worlds does not mean for him that, like a Buddhist disciple in *nirvāṇa,* he disappears sounding out among the harmonies of the starry cosmos, but that he takes with him into those cosmic harmonies his 'I' and the conscious memory of all the associations of his earthly life, the ties which united him to all he loved. And so he remains, even when absorbed into the starry harmonies, a conscious 'I' and, as an 'I', a creative member of the cosmos, taking his share in all the further for-

[*] *Cf.* Rudolf Steiner, *Knowledge of the Higher Worlds* [GA 10], the chapter [10] on 'The Guardian of the Threshold'.

[†] *Cf. Ursprung,* 37.

[‡] *Ursprung,* 57.

mations of the Earth, in the building of the temple of mankind, until at length the Earth itself is once more absorbed into the harmonies of the cosmos.

The Creation of Man

In this divine archetypal picture of humanity the pupil of the Christ-path at the same time finds the Mystery of the divine primordial creation, the crown of which is that human picture: 'And the Godhead of the Elohim created man after their own image, in the divine image they created him.'* What Buddha finds under the Tree of Knowledge, or at least what he reveals of it to humanity, is only the third creation, Lucifer's creation. Christ leads beyond this to the Elohim creation. Moses, to whom the cosmic Christ was revealed in the Burning Bush—for at that time He was not yet the earthly Christ—was led by Him through the Mystery of Yahveh's creation to that Mystery of the archetypal creation that he was able to proclaim in the Book of Genesis. Buddha only knows the (Luciferic) human being, 'who has to be overcome'. Moses divined in his vision the human being of the primordial creation by the Elohim, the divine future picture of man, that being of the youngest hierarchy. It is the permanent greatness in his words (Gen. 1:27), how he divines the archetypal connection of the human being with the divine in the world and presents it to us; he recognises how the Gods looked beyond themselves when they created man, by concentrating their own being to a higher synthesis. As a consequence of the impact of other powers, this divine archetype did not become earthly reality. But in the light of Christ we learn to understand again the mystery of Man in connection with those Mysteries of the Gods that are sealed within the primordial creation.

Becoming Human

With regard to the Buddha, an account attempting to be objective aims not only to show on the one hand how distant he still was from these mysteries, but on the other hand also how closely he did approach them. For everywhere we regard Buddha not only as the pre-Christian counterpart, but in certain respects as the forerunner and messenger of Christ (see above p. 15). It could probably be said that Buddha actually

* *Ibid.* 13ff., and 22–26.

no longer beheld—or not yet beheld—the human being as the gods had created him in the primordial beginning, had not taken into account the full human meaning Christ gave to the word 'human being'. In his proclamation he recognises or takes into account actually only the connection human beings have with the Luciferic being, not the connection he has with the progressing Hierarchies of earthly development, with the divine. It has rightly been indicated how those gods, too, that still lead a living presence in the earlier religion of the Vedas pale in Buddha's teaching.

Yet on the other hand it is true that the gods who in Buddhism disappear as it were into the periphery regain a real existence in the inner centre in the meditation of Buddha, that in this meditation also the connection of the human being with the gods—or angels, as one more accessibly says today—in a certain way is again experienced. Buddha sees initially only the Luciferic element in the human being. But then he is the one who under the Tree of Knowledge of Lucifer—in the meditation of the sacred night—overcomes the Luciferic being, or, as it is expressed in the pictorial language of the legend, causes the army of Mara to flee. And all the divine host, all the hosts of angels bow before the victorious conqueror, the perfected Buddha—in the same way as, according to the legend, symbolically meaningful, once in the temple, the divine images already bowed before the Buddha-child (see above, p. 25). In this in particular there lies something magnificent, how with Buddha it is in a certain sense recognised here that the human being is more than all the angelic Hierarchies, that when he has raised himself—to the heights of his being—reachable through the path of meditation, all the gods who hitherto have guided him now serve him. For the gods themselves, in order to become Buddhas, would have to descend from their heavenly spheres to human incarnation. Only in a human body, as Buddha knew and taught, can they achieve the highest of all aims of being, that of a perfected Buddha. Consequently, in Buddha's teaching, human birth counts as the most eminent of all births; for human beings from the earthly point of view, the entry into the bliss of the heavenly world is called the 'good journey'. In the same way for the gods, from the viewpoint of the higher worlds, a human incarnation is the 'good journey'.*

This is the only time that Buddha speaks in such a way about the

* Itivuttaka 83; see H. B. *Buddha*, Germ. ed. II, 62f. *Cf.* this what is said above in footnote on p. 15.

human being, almost the only time where he speaks about the human being as such (see above, p. 4). And here, too, the human being, although divined, is not yet fully seen in a Christianised sense. Here too the 'I' is still missing, the divine prototype, the image of the gods, the aim of the gods creatively realised in earthly activity. The exalted aim of Buddha, for the arriving at which the gods themselves have to descend to a human birth, is again only a negative aim; it has to do here with the severing of incarnation, of that ego-less extinguishing or dissolution into the star-harmonies of the cosmos that can only be reached through a human incarnation.

Out of all of this it clearly arises that, when Buddha's teaching had later become the Buddhist religion, the divine beings do not play the same role as in other religions. The Buddhist humanity of Asia does look up to the gods, but to the human being who has become knowledgeable, the redeemed and redeeming human being, to the *Übermensch*, the 'overhuman', the superman, the Buddha. Buddha does not speak of a religious veneration of the gods, but only of the way how gods, how angels, as well as spiritual beings in general, are experienced in meditation, how they are met on the path of meditation. Through the pictorial consciousness, the meditative life, also with Buddha, slowly penetrates towards the world's essential being. Buddha openly relates* how before his becoming a Buddha, he was elevated step by step to a purification of his vision. At first he sees only a glow. After a time, he beholds figures and colours. On a further level he can also converse with spiritual beings, who announce themselves through these shapes and colours, yet he is still unable to recognise to which angelic hierarchy the being belongs. Through continuing the meditative exertion he also gains this knowledge. By further purifying what he found in his vision during meditation, it finally becomes clear through what deed of destiny, through what *karma,* those beings have risen to their present stage in the development of the world—which is the content of their consciousness—and whether he had a relationship to them in an earlier life. Finally, he is able to dip completely into the consciousness of these beings. What shines through this narration of Buddha is nothing other than what one had in both the earlier and the newer Mysteries as stages of higher knowledge, above sensory knowledge.

---

* Aṅguttaranikāya Vol. IV, p. 252ff. (Pali Text Society edition). On this see H. B. *Buddha,* II, 55f.

- Firstly, a stage of picture consciousness, of Imagination, of beholding colours and forms,
- secondly a recognising of the spiritual beings behind the pictures (the stage of Inspiration);
- thirdly, a dipping into these spiritual beings with one's own consciousness (the stage of Intuition).*

Meditation leads to the experience of the advanced divine being, the good angel; the disciple of Buddha is also led to a real experience of the fiend among the gods and the adversary of human nature. This being is in particular also the adversary of meditation itself and always attempts to disturb it. It is called Mara the tempter. The attempt to raise oneself in meditation always calls up Mara the tempter to resist. After the Bodhisattva, during the sacred night in which he became the Buddha, entered the 'sphere of enlightenment' and had sat under the sacred fig tree for the final decisive meditation, he himself challenged Mara the tempter to battle and sent his demonic host to flight. This struggle of Buddha with Mara is portrayed in the legends of the Buddha in gruesome, lurid pictures.† But since the heart of the Holy One is completely protected by love, no weapon can harm him; the poisoned darts remain hovering above his head, transforming into wreaths of flowers through the power of his love.

After the baptism in the Jordan, Christ-Jesus was tempted by the devil in the wilderness. Buddha, too, in decisive moments of his life, encountered Mara the tempter. The tempter says to Jesus: 'If you are the Son of God, tell these stones to become bread' (Matt. 4:3 NIV [*cf.* Luke 4:3]). 'Again, the devil took him to a very high mountain and showed him all the kingdoms of the world and their splendour. "All this I will give you," he said, "if you will bow down and worship me"' (Matt. 4:8f. [*cf.* Luke 4:5–7]). The second of these two temptations recalls the offer to rule the world with which Mara approaches the one who precisely gives up worldly life, the Bodhisattva who rides out of his father's palace during the night.‡ The changing of stones into bread recalls the demand of Mara to the Bodhisattva in the time before his

* *Cf.* with much else as a continuation of *Knowledge of the Higher Worlds,* the publication '*Die Stufen der höheren Erkenntnis*' in Lucifer-Gnosis, No. 34 [1904. GA 12; Tb 641]. Eng. tr. *The Stages of Higher Knowledge.* Tr. L.D. Monges & F. McKnight. Spring Valley, New York: Anthroposophic Press 1974/81. Online:
http://wn.rsarchive.org/Books/GA012/English/AP1967/GA012_index.html.

† H. B. *Buddha,* I, 57ff.

‡ Nidānakathā, 63, not contained in *Lalitavistara* (touched on in H. B. *Buddha*).

enlightenment, weakened through asceticism, to break his strict fasting and take nourishment again.[*] There is no convincing corresponding temptation to the third[†] temptation of Christ, on the pinnacle of the Temple—Matt. 4:5f. [*cf.* Luke 4:9f.]: 'Then the devil took him to the holy city and had him stand on the highest point of the temple. "If you are the Son of God," he said, "throw yourself down: for it is written ..."' *etc.* Even the other two lack the deeper connections to the story of the temptation of Christ.

The figure itself of Mara, however, closely resembles the tempter of Christ. The two sides of the adversary, the Luciferic and the Ahrimanic, are also indicated with Buddha, when Mara is presented first as the demonic tempter to sensuality, then as the Lord of Death.[‡] But with Buddha the Luciferic temptation to sensuality and desire is indeed overcome; the Indian can only attempt to escape the Ahrimanic power of death by severing birth through overcoming the desire for existence. Even the story of the temptation of Christ—as Rudolf Steiner points out in his lecture-course in Christiania[§]—does not yet signify the decisive victory over the Ahrimanic being. Only on the cross of Golgotha is the decisive victory achieved; the power of death, the might of Ahriman is overcome. And what takes place on the cross of Golgotha, that is, as far as otherwise the parallels can be drawn, always that which is added as the new thing in Christianity, to that which in a certain manner can also be found with Buddha.

Moreover, as the Bodhisattva awakening to Buddhahood under the Bodhi tree achieves the decisive victory over Mara-Lucifer, he repeatedly afflicts the perfected Buddha with his whisperings. We know the scene in the account of Buddha's death, where Mara-Lucifer repeatedly tries, through enticingly mentioning *nirvāṇa*, to make Buddha prematurely break off his earthly task, to disappear from the Earth (see above, p. 34).

The disciple struggling for meditation has to stand up afresh repeatedly to the temptation of this demon of sensuality. For through meditation the realm of the senses is superseded, in which Mara is the lord and master. Consequently, he has every reason to resist such a

---

[*] H. B. *Buddha*, I, 54.

[†] The third temptation in Luke's order; the second in Matthew's—*Tr. note.*

[‡] *Ibid.* II, 67.

[§] Rudolf Steiner, *The Fifth Gospel*, lecture-cycle, Christiania, 1–6 Oct. 1913 [see lecture 5] and Cologne, 17–18 Dec. 1913 [GA 148].

superseding. If the meditation is successful, the Buddhist texts say, then the disciple rests in a secure fortress, in which the might of the fiend can no longer do anything to him.* Continuous awake consciousness is the inner attitude, through which the disciple most surely encounters the temptations of Mara. For this reason a circumspect consciousness is the essential requirement of a true meditation, already intended in the Eightfold Path. Here 'right mindfulness' or 'right concentration', and 'right reflection' or 'right meditation' are directly presupposed. Christ in Gethsemane calls the sleeping disciples to 'watch and pray'; Buddha repeatedly admonishes his disciples to retain this awake concentration and reflective consciousness. He Himself preserves this concentrated consciousness in all life-situations until death. The legend tells how already as a child the Bodhisattva, too, everywhere preserved this circumspection, indeed how he entered the earthly womb 'circumspectly and consciously'. One does not need to take this literally in an external sense, yet one recognises what value Buddha gave to the carrying of full inner consciousness throughout all the stages and tasks of life. In the large section on the Path (see above p. 55) this was discussed in detail. Even a holding on to consciousness during sleep—we find this developed further in *Knowledge of the Higher Worlds* as a 'continuity of consciousness'—is already gently indicated. Buddha, not yet focusing on what only in Christ is re-won as the constant and eternal 'I', nevertheless leads in this direction through the commandment for inner full consciousness. In this the 'I' is found in Christ. We can also say the early Vedic Indian knew the higher 'I' or self (*ātman*)—though not yet fully consciously, yet nevertheless in a dreaming consciousness of atavistic clairvoyance. Buddha advances to inner full consciousness, yet he does not find therein the 'I'. This was first achieved again afresh by Christ. The true higher 'I' is only found on the Christian path where previously the meeting with the 'Guardian of the Threshold' is experienced.

Thus Mara's essential being stands in a clear inner connection with the essence of meditation. Thus essentially he was experienced by the early Indians in meditation. The experiences contain the full Christ-depths only when on the way from Buddha to Christ the advancing soul glimpses the figure of Christ, how he keeps the balance between the power of temptation to the right and to the left. In the statue of Christ, meant for the Goetheanum in Dornach, Switzerland that was

---

* *Ibid.* II, 65f.

destroyed by fire,[*] this tremendous cosmic Imagination was to find its sculptural expression.

Meditation as a Path

It is a characteristic of Indian spiritual life that since primordial times, much more than in the cultures of other areas of the Earth, the comprehensive significance of meditation for spiritual development has been recognised. It is indeed practised in other cultures, even in the West, only by much smaller groups. But nowhere was and is the spiritual atmosphere of a whole earthly region so filled and penetrated by meditation as is India. In no other land is this area of human spiritual life so organised and methodically researched than there. Since early times in India, the name for this methodically practiced exercise of meditation was Yoga. Out of this ancient Yoga Buddha in his Path took over in a purer form the quintessence of what was spiritually worked at there. And Buddha's path is a path of meditation.[†] When here it is attempted also to show what the significance the step from Buddha to Christ means for the path of meditation, the advance therein is one side of the account. The other side is this, to show what it means when, precisely out of the richness of what was gained in India and ultimately through Buddha, the step from Buddha to Christ is taken.

At the beginning of the meditative beholding there stands, as Buddha's experience with the gods has already shown (see above, p. 64),

[*] On New Year's Eve 1922. The sculpture that was still in Rudolf Steiner's studio was consequently preserved. It is now housed in the Second Goetheanum with other artistic items, including a complete scale model of the First Goetheanum—*Tr. note.*

[†] In the scheme of the Path of the Dīghanikāya, meditation, the second of four stages is what gives the whole Path its character. The scheme of the Eightfold Path climaxes in 'right concentration', that is, meditation, for the previous seven members are the moral preparation. With all the inner relationship of Buddha's path to the Yoga path of meditation, it has to be emphasised that breathing exercises, so important in ancient Yoga, completely step back with Buddha. It is only said that the awake consciousness that penetrates all bodily tasks, should also embrace the breathing. Likewise, what is called the 'seat' (*āsana*) in ancient Yoga, the complicated bodily positions, no longer plays a decisive role in Buddhist meditation as it did in ancient Yoga. The focus with Buddha rests on the spirituality of the meditation and for the moral purification serving as preparation for meditation.

also with the Path of Buddha, that picture which forms out of light and colour. The consciousness of the one who meditates becomes picture-consciousness, Imagination. Buddha himself, who speaks more abstractly when he wants to communicate knowledge, immediately uses pictures when he enlarges on the essence of the Path. Already with the word 'path', as we saw, a significant picture is presented, painted more in detail by Buddha as the wandering over rough mountain paths. On these, like an unskillful cow in the mountains, the wanderer who is without right inner orientation and moral purification, seeking the path of meditation out of mere inquisitiveness gets lost.

In one of Buddha's sermons,* there is a pictorial description of inner development that takes place in the advancing meditation, and of the part which the beings of the spiritual world, the hierarchies of angels, take towards this development. No longer in the physical realm, we feel, lie the things about which Buddha speaks, but in the realm of the etheric, of the tender etheric organs that are formed in the practice of meditation. We also find with Buddha the picture of growing plants, which has been presented in all the Mysteries for the mystery of the burgeoning etheric, the life of growth and development.† In order not to remove the fragrance that belongs directly to everything pictorial, let us allow the pictures in Buddha's words simply to make their effect:

> In Indra's paradise, O disciples, there stands a wonderful tree, the growth of which the gods accompany with interest. When they perceive the first light green shoots of the leaves, then they eagerly look forward to the soon fully developed leaves. Full of expectation they see the beginning of the first tender buds of the blossoms and rejoice when soon the swelling and then the opened bud follows. Then they wait for the fully revealed flowers, and when at last the whole tree stands in full blossom, then they celebrate under the tree of the gods throughout four divine months a heavenly feast of rejoicing with everything that pleases the senses, and the blossoming tree spreads out radiating beams of light and its scent fills the whole circumference of the sky. This growth of the divine tree, you disciples, is as follows: if the pupil of the spirit inwardly decides for the path, which leads him out of his homeland into homelessness, then the tree of the gods begins to produce its first light green shoots. When he then follows his decision and puts on the garments of the monk, then the

* Aṅguttaranikāya Vol. IV, p. 117, see H. B. *Buddha*, II, 61f.

† Also in the book *Knowledge of the Higher Worlds*, Germ. 6th ed. p. 41, it is emphasised, how in the higher worlds, of all natural beings it is plants that mostly resemble their physical composition.

> tree develops its leaves. If the pupil then reaches the first level of meditation, then the first tender beginnings of the flowering buds are formed. In the second level of meditation the buds are further developed, and in the third they begin to open. When the fourth level of meditation is reached, the blossom begins to be fully revealed and when finally in *nirvāṇa* all earthly darkening is purified away, the redemption of the heart and the redemption of the will has been found by the disciple, then the divine tree in Indra's paradise stands in full blossom and one angelic hierarchy proclaim the happy event to the other, and the jubilation rises up to the gods of the Brahmā heaven.

As we saw, the disciple of Buddha did not approach the 'I', hence the pictorial world of the supersensory astral element is revealed to his vision more richly. We could say the Christian path is more oriented towards the 'I', towards the side of the will, the Buddhist path more towards that etheric element and with this at the same time towards cosmic thinking, towards knowledge. These four stages of meditation are also described in pictures of the etheric element as something fundamental, as presented in Buddha's sermon quoted above, and elsewhere.* They are the same four stages through which Buddha under the Bodhi tree penetrates to enlightenment after the victory over Mara. This victory over Mara precedes the actual attainment of the situation of meditation. From everything he still has of hidden worldly lusts, what still remains of enmity and hate, heaviness and sleepiness, anxiety and disquiet, of doubt of all kinds, has to be purified by the disciple of Buddha before he enters the sacred sphere of meditation.

In the legend of the Buddha, the enemy of the soul appears as the hosts of Mara, which Buddha under the Bodhi tree sent in flight. If the one seeking meditation has inwardly liberated himself from this, he experiences this inner liberation in pictures. He feels, it is said, as one who has settled an oppressive debt, or recovered from a painful illness, or been released from prison or bondage, or as one who has luckily found his way again out of a bleak and dangerous forest wilderness to a safe and homely village. In these pictures there still lives a one-sided, characteristic Indo-Buddhist joy of liberation from the weight of what is earthly. The feeling is present that more is seen of this personal liberation than of the earthly element from which one has become free, but which furthermore comes to a stop as unredeemed in darkness

* H. B. *Buddha*, II, 44ff.

within his circuit. This Buddhist meditation, which only aims for personal liberation and feels superearthly bliss therein, is different from the Christian, Johannine meditation. The latter, moreover, taking on those destinies of the earthly element, leads right through apocalyptic horrors. Yet here already Mahayana Buddhism (see p. 14f.) has taken a further step by setting up the fundamental statement: 'All the suffering of the whole world I will bear in my own consciousness.' Precisely this basic sentence characterises the system under discussion as the 'Great Path' (literally, 'Great Vehicle'), *mahāyāna*, in contrast to the earlier individual path of Buddha as *hinayāna*, the 'Small Path' or 'Smaller Vehicle'.

The four stages of meditation themselves are so experienced in the Buddhist pictorial consciousness that a feeling of bliss is felt, which passes over to the higher stages in an increasing peace and equanimity, purity and splendour.

- At the first stage, the picture before the consciousness is still somewhat plain and prosaic, that of an artificially produced effervescence.
- At the second stage, in which every mental picture of outer objects (still present with the first stage) disappears, the person meditating has the picture of a cool stream, which has a source within a lake that is not filled by outer tributaries.
- At the third stage a feeling of bliss that is sublime above all the riots of desire, is accompanied by the picture of a pond of lotuses, in which the lotus flowers, without reaching the surface of the water, are completely bathed by cool water.
- Finally, at the fourth stage, where the one meditating abides in complete solitude (cf. above, p. 12) and his whole body is rayed through by purity and splendour [*Helle*—luminous clarity], sees himself in imagination clothed with a white garment that covers him from head to foot, so that not the smallest part of the body is left uncovered by whiteness.

Inner transition

These pictures of Buddhist meditation-experience partly recall those of Christian meditation. Here, though, the differences are to be noticed, and also what is the same or similar in certain finer details, those which are precisely founded on the inner transition from Buddha to Christ. Thus we find the 'white garment' of the pure, light-filled etheric element probably wherever a specific stage of meditative, priestly experience is achieved. And yet one feels, the disciple of Buddha thereby beholds only his purity and separation from everything earthly. Even more than this, we feel a beholding of martyrdom, a suffering for the earthly element, where we encounter almost the same picture in the words of the Apocalyptist:

> He who overcomes will, like them, be dressed in white. I will never blot out his name from the book of life (Rev. 3:5),

and in particular in the following:

> These are they who have come out of the great tribulation; they have washed their robes and made them white [Luther translates: *helle gemacht*] in the blood of the Lamb. Therefore,
>
> they are before the throne of God and serve him day and night in his temple;
> and he who sits on the throne will spread his tent over them.
> Never again will they hunger; never again will they thirst.
> The sun will not beat upon them, nor any scorching heat.
> For the Lamb at the centre of the throne will be their shepherd;
> he will lead them to springs of living water.
> And God will wipe away every tear from their eyes (Rev. 7:14–17 NIV).

Other differences and nuances are also significant. It corresponds to the Buddhist path when as a picture of higher consciousness the lotus-flower bathed by cool water is presented to us. Water pictures the etheric element; the picture of the lotus-flower bathed in water—which still completely weaves in the etheric element, not yet the physical element—has not yet found its way to the Earth and not yet to the 'I'. If we want to build up a picture out of a Christian consciousness adequate for this consciousness, then instead of the lotus-flower we would have to choose the picture of the rose rooted in the ground. We could think of the beautiful words* of the poet Albert Steffen, in *Wegzehrung* ('Provisions for the way'):

> *Die Erde ward für dich zum Heiligtume,*
> *du wurzelst fest, du willst nicht fort von ihr.*
> *Ich aber sehne mich, ich darbe hier,*
> *Ich such im All nach meinem Eigentume.*
>
> *Du überwächst den Tod mit deinen Farben*
> *und saugst dir ewiges Leben aus dem Boden.*
> *Ich kehre immer wieder, um zu sterben.*

*From '*An eine Rose*'. Albert Steffen, *Wegzehrung*, Dornach, 1964[5], 60.

Denn ach: Nur durch mein Suchen, Sehnen, Darben,
nur durch die Wiederkehr von vielen Toden,
darf ich um dich, o rote Rose, werben.

The Earth became for you a sanctuary,
You, firmly rooted, do not want to escape from her.
But I, full of longing, I am in want here;
I seek in the universe for that which is mine.

You grow beyond death with your colours
and draw eternal life out of the ground.
I return repeatedly in order to die.

For oh! Only through my seeking, longing and falling short,
only through the return of many deaths,
may I attempt to woo you, O red rose.

It is the picture of the rose that in Goethe's poetic fragment '*Die Geheimnisse*' ['The Mysteries'] is profoundly connected with the other picture expressing most of all that which is foreign to Buddhism. In the picture of the cross, which belongs to Christianity, we behold what the earthly, physical element is, what death is and what space and time is. Buddhism knows only the picture—now for the last time—of the Bodhi tree. It shrinks back from the picture of death in the arid wood of the cross. But death itself is overcome through Christ on Golgotha. It is changed again into life; the arid wood of the cross is clad again with burgeoning life. This is then beheld again in the Imagination of the Rosy Cross (see above in Chapter 1, p. 13).* This picture of the Rosy Cross, consequently, belongs to the Christian path, as the lotus-flower does to the Indian path.

If we follow a little further the experience of pictures on the Buddhist path, we arrive at that point that was and is significant for all paths of initiation: the loosening of the etheric body from the physical that carries the imprint of the organs of the astral body. We can expect that in India, where the experience of the etheric was particularly strong, this loosening of the etheric from the physical was also raised to a characteristic pictorial experience. It does stand there—and the section on the Path in the Dīghanikāya shows all this in words. The peculiar rhythms and rhythmic repetitions in the original language manifest the

---

*On the rose-cross, see especially Rudolf Steiner, *Esoteric/ Occult Science* [GA 13], Chapter 5 on '*Knowledge of Higher Worlds*', and the lecture-course *The Gospel of St John* (Cassel, 1909), lecture 1 [GA 112].

etheric streams—before the spiritual eyes of the disciple initially the connection of the physical or physical-etheric and of the astral body in the picture of a 'pure spotless polished eight-sided precious stone', and of a coloured thread passing through it.[*] Then, we read further, it forms a spiritual-etheric body with all its members and equipped complete with all the sensory organs. This body he withdraws out of the physical-etheric body. The picture before the imagination is that of withdrawing of a reed out of its case, or a sword out of its sheath, or a snake out of its basket. The first of these three pictures was an ancient picture of the Indian Mystery tradition, mentioned already in the Kathaka Upanishad.

In this spiritual-etheric body the disciple of the Buddhist path had the instrument to practise what is called the arts of the super-earthly power (*iddhi*). It is the same super-earthly power that Buddha explained to his disciple Ananda. Whoever masters its elements would have the capability to stay in existence until the end of the earthly age (see above, p. 33). These elements, as we saw, are will, courage, power of thinking and the ability to fashion pictorial thought; the way to achieve this is none other than the 'Path' itself. As the potter fashions impressionable clay, or as the ivory-cutter or the goldsmith works on his material, so works the initiate, we read, into the substance of his spiritual-etheric body.[†] And wonderful are the achievements which this higher spiritual-bodily instrument enables him to perform. We are told he can multiply his appearances—appearing in a phantom-body now here now there, as is often said of Indian fakirs[‡]—make himself

---

[*] With this it is remarkable that the physical body, which in the same text immediately preceding is described as the entity 'built out of the four elements, presenting the result of the physical heredity, bearing the conditions of decay and of redemption in itself', is then seen in the picture of the 'pure, spotless, eight-sided precious stone', that, no doubt, is the diamond. It is as if for those higher Christian mysteries, for the transformation even of the physical body, Buddha's age was not yet ripe. Here in the Indian account of Buddha's Path, there shine in somehow like a premonition the mysteries of transforming that which in the human being is still carbon-like into that which is like a diamond.

[†] H. B. *Buddha*, II, 73.

[‡] Readers of Rudyard Kipling's immortal novel (Beckh calls it «his amiable novel», *Festschrift*, 39) *Kim* (1901)—Kim, 'the little friend of all the world' with an Irish father and Indian mother, is himself an offspring of a union of West & East, with its sinister figure Lurgan Sahib, the master-spy with remarkable faculties—may be interested in Peter Hopkirk, *Quest for Kim: in Search of Kipling's Great Game*, London: John Murray, 1996. Hopkirk describes his search for the possible real-life personages, who emerge as interesting and mysterious as their fictional counterparts—*Tr. note.*

invisible, elevate himself over the earth, walk on water as on the earth, and stretch his spiritual-etheric organs over long distances. Specific abilities of clairvoyance, of perceiving cosmic harmonies, of seeing through the thoughts of strangers, can be listed. What is said here of the overcoming of gravity through ether forces*—in Buddhism this overcoming of earthly gravity must have played a special role—recalls what is called levitation with many mystics.

We find this etheric phenomenon amongst what are called the 'miracles' of Jesus, as told in the Christian Gospels. Thus, for example, the multiple appearances, John 6:25;† the walking on the water, Matt. 14, Mark 6, John 6. In the realm of the etheric forces, to which the Mystery-path of Buddha points here, the power of Christ is the highest, the power of the Sun. The highest rays which work directly through Buddha are those of Venus-Mercury. Phenomena that in a certain manner extend over the whole Earth, which can also flow out of atavistic forces, are somewhat different in the light of the power of the Christ-Sun. One can compare precisely the apparent similarity between these Buddhist *iddhi*-phenomena and what is in the Christian Gospels, the differences already here and there in the nuances of the descriptions. In the Buddhist text the description rests on the one hand very much on the externals of the phenomena, and on the other hand it touches on the sensational, fakir aspect. With this we feel old atavistic forces in their decadence, that which was still there in early India, the decreasing forces of the Tree of Life.

Walking on the water

Let us stay with what is said of Buddha concerning walking on the water, the way it is said compared with the narration in the Christian Gospel. There we find, whether we read in Matthew, Mark or John, and quite apart from everything else that raises the whole event to a much higher cosmic and at the same time moral niveau, two words of cosmically profound significance in the mouth of Christ-Jesus. These two words, in which everything is enclosed, that we can also feel as the step from Buddha to Christ, are the words 'I am'. The whole event in the

* *Cf.* on this Günther Wachsmuth, *Die ätherischen Bildekräfte in Kosmos, Erde und Mensch*, which explains gravity out of the mystery of the four kinds of ether, p. 86ff. [Eng. tr. *The Etheric Formative Forces in Cosmos, Earth and Man*. London/ New York, 1932. 78ff. Online from: https://www.scribd.com]

† On this, see Rudolf Steiner, *The Gospel of St John* (Cassel, 1909), lecture 10 [GA 112].

Christian Gospel is raised out of the sphere of what is only the etheric element, in which it stands with Buddha, into the 'I'-sphere, into the I-am sphere. (To explain: it is assumed that when in the Gospels it says of Jesus that 'he prayed', nothing else is meant than the Christian sense of what with Buddha is called meditation.)

> (Matt. 14:23–32. AV/KJV rev.) And when he had sent the multitudes away, he went up into a mountain apart to pray: and when the evening was come, he was there alone. But the ship was now in the midst of the sea, tossed with waves: for the wind was contrary. And in the fourth watch of the night Jesus went unto them, walking on the sea. And when the disciples saw him walking on the sea, they were troubled, saying, It is a ghost! and they cried out for fear. But straightway Jesus spake unto them, saying, Be of good cheer; I AM, be not afraid. And Peter answered him and said, Lord, if it be thou, bid me come unto thee on the water. And he said, Come. And when Peter was come down out of the ship, he walked on the water, to go to Jesus. But when he saw the wind boisterous, he was afraid; and beginning to sink, he cried, saying, Lord, save me. And immediately Jesus stretched forth his hand, and caught him, and said unto him, O thou of little faith, wherefore didst thou doubt? And when they were come into the ship, the wind ceased. Then they that were in the ship came and worshipped him, saying, Of a truth thou art the Son of God.

The tremendous thing about the Gospel narration lies in how the cosmic ether-forces of Christ commanding the wind and the waves unites morally with the cosmic strength of the 'I' and the human forces of the heart. And someone imaginatively experiencing the whole event in meditation unites the strength of the 'I' with the power of the ether, whereas through the Buddhist meditation only ether-forces are awoken.

The Rosy Cross and the Holy Grail

Only etheric life weaves in the pictures of the Buddhist path of meditation. 'I'-strength lives in that which is beheld in a similar manner on the Christian path. It lives strongly in the death picture of the cross, in which Christian thinking and Christian devotion have from early on found their focus. It lives more strongly where* 'shining roses surround

*Words spoken by Felix Balde in *The Guardian of the Threshold,* Scene 1. Rudolf Steiner, *Four Mystery Plays* [GA 14]. Tr. Adam Bittleston. London: Rudolf Steiner Press, 1982. 260.

with deep significance the sign of death', where 'I'-strength unites with ether-strength, in the Rosy Cross. We have often mentioned this, to which the words of Rudolf Steiner* relate:

> Someone who knows the mystery of the Holy Grail knows that out of the wood of the cross the living, burgeoning life proceeds, the immortal 'I', that is symbolised through the roses around the black wood of the cross.

And 'I'-strength lives probably most strongly in the picture that has just been mentioned and already presented before us in connection with the Rosy Cross, in that picture that so aptly is the Imagination of the development of our consciousness-soul† today, in the picture of the Holy Grail. The mystery of the 'I' in its connection with the most profound Mysteries of the blood lives, as in the Rosy Cross, so also in the picture of the Holy Grail, in which the precious stone that slipped out of Lucifer's crown became the vessel for the Redeemer's blood. And in it lives the Mystery of the consciousness-soul, which is to receive the highest cosmic 'I'. All the lunar power of knowledge—thus the picture speaks to us—is to become the pure vessel, which takes up the cosmic Sun-'I', the Christ.

Like a rich, luxuriant floral garden, a magic garden, the pictorial world of the Indian, Buddhist meditation stands before us. But none of the flowers that we find there, in fragrance and sublimity, in world-renewing strength, achieves the picture of the Holy Grail. This one picture weighs for the soul more than the whole pictorial world of the Indian floral garden. It can only be found when in our meditation we inwardly advance from Buddha to Christ.

That we do not find this picture of the Grail with Buddha—as in India generally—cannot cause wonder, after all that has resulted on the

---

* Rudolf Steiner, *The Gospel of St John* (Cassel, 1909), lecture 1 [GA 112].

† 'Consciousness-soul', or 'spiritual soul', is the term in spiritual science for the third differentiation of the triune soul. For the individual, in reflecting upon experience, the *spirit lights up*, the realisation of the eternal element, for 'what is really true neither arises nor passes away' (Rudolf Steiner, *Theosophy*, GA 9). It is particularly developed in the seven-year period, age 35–42; in European history it came to birth in the late Middle Ages and Renaissance with the birth of 'onlooker consciousness', typified in Shakespeare's *Hamlet*. One can also point to the birth of natural science, the voyages of discovery, the development of national states, of the major-minor system in music, the phenomena of perspective in the fine arts, and the many phenomena of a growing awareness of the many issues hinging on human responsibilities, and so on—*Tr. note*.

one side concerning the relationship of Buddha to the 'I'-impulse, and on the other side of the Holy Grail to the same impulse. At least this applies to that glimpse of the Grail that sees therein the vessel in which the blood of the Redeemer was received on Golgotha. How can a picture that contains the secret of Golgotha, be such before Golgotha itself had taken place?

Now, there is alongside the Easter-view of the Grail still another, which we find with Wolfram von Eschenbach and can call the Christmas-glimpse of the Grail,[*] the picture of the precious stone carried down by hosts of angels from starry heights. An echo of this is also in the Buddhist Christmas-story in that bowl of beryl, in which the Bodhisattva before his birth rests in the body of the Queen Maya, and in the other which the god Brahmā presented as a gift to the child. The Holy Grail is also beheld many times as a bowl of beryl. There is a legend according to which among the treasures which the Queen of Sheba presented to [King] Solomon, such a bowl of beryl or emerald was to be found. In the Buddha legend (*Lalitavistara*) the picture is painted[†] in the following way:

> He himself, the Bodhisattva, rests in his mother's womb in the meditating position. In order that no earthly impurity may soil him, he is surrounded by a sparkling shell of radiant beryl, which after the birth is taken by gods (angels) into the *Brahmā* heaven and kept there as a sacred reliquary. In the night during which the Bodhisattva enters the womb a lotus plant grows out of the earth reaching to the *Brahmā* heaven. Only *Brahmā* is able to behold this lotus. What exists in the wide world-all full of strength in its essence unites in this lotus as a drop of honey. *Brahmā* himself offers to the child in the womb this drop of honey in a chalice made of beryl. Nobody would be able to bear this drop of strength except the Bodhisattva now in this his last incarnation, who in his various existences did not tire to offer soothing relief to help suffering beings.

The earlier Path

For Buddha—as in general in Indian Yoga—all those visions of the Imaginative consciousness and all those *iddhi*-forces are not somehow the aim of the path, but only signs that the one who is treading the path of meditation has reached a certain stage. Through clairaudience (perceiving the cosmic harmonies) and recognising the thoughts of

---

[*] *Cf.* H. B. *Our Origin in the Light*, footnote 1 (forthcoming).

[†] H. B. *Buddha*, I, 34.

others (looking into the hearts of human beings)* the Path leads further to knowledge, that is, to the three Noble Truths of Buddha, which have already been presented in Chapter 3 above. Only on this high level does the disciple attain them as a knowledge that really beholds, which is more than only abstract knowledge and mere belief. This knowledge is the third of the four great stages on the Path (see above, p. 56). Through this the actual goal is then reached, the fourth stage, the stage of emancipation, or *nirvāṇa*.

The knowledge of suffering, too, which until then is always presented abstractly, becomes pictorial when in the inner development of the Path, through the unfolding of the higher spirit-organ, one progresses towards it. Then it no longer simply means, 'Birth is suffering, age is suffering, illness is suffering, death is suffering ... the origin of suffering is *taṇhā*, thirsting longing ..., the end of suffering, emancipation from *taṇhā*', *etc.* But in a picture all this stands before the spiritual eye of the beholder, in the picture of the pure, clear mountain-lake, in which one can see right to the bottom, where a good eye can perceive pearly shells, pebbles and shoals of fish. We say to ourselves: this is the pure, clear mountain-lake, these are the pebble-stones and pearly shells on its bottom and shoals of fishes that live in it. In the same way the one who meditates comes to realise when, in pure concentration, he steers his thoughts, which have become pictorial and no longer darkened through earthly passion, towards the destruction of earthly delusion: this is suffering, this is the origin and annihilation of suffering, this the path leading to the annihilation of suffering. This visionary knowledge gives him the inner emancipation, in which he then knows, 'this is the emancipation; birth is annihilated, the holy life is perfected, duty is fulfilled, earthly things are finished'.

For the whole substance of Buddhist knowledge of the world, this picture is one of the most significant, bringing the most light. Only like an overclouding that passes, like sea-shells or little fishes at the bottom of a mountain-lake, the earthly element swims in the crystal-clear purity of the cosmic ether. Buddha only looks on this crystal-clear purity of the cosmic element, of *nirvāṇa*, of 'nothingness', as one says from the earthly point of view, as that which is the only true and real. Through the deceiving, seeming reality of the earthly element, that crystal-clear purity is clouded in passing. But everything earthly, compared to that crystal-clear purity, is something without being. It is

* *Ibid.* II, 77f.

consequently the earnest wish of the disciple of Buddha to renounce as soon as possible this non-being, this clouding of the earthly element, in order again to expand, to dive into and to dissolve again in that crystal-clear purity of *nirvāṇa*. This dissolving is called *parinirvāṇa*.

We feel the sublimity of all these pictures and imaginations, but at the same time we have to recognise their essential difference from the facts of Christianity. Buddha is only interested in the crystal-like purity of the clear mountain-lake. He finds that the earthly ground of the lake is obscure. There powers of darkness reign, powers of death. Before them he turns away. He does not get to the bottom, to the earthly element, to the 'I'; he remains with the water, the etheric element. Christ reaches the ground. He goes through the earthly element, connecting to the Earth, wrestles in it with the powers of darkness and death and overcomes them. Through this He purifies and transforms the element of the Earth, he lays the seed into the Earth through which at the end of the great process of transformation and purification of development the Earth once again can be taken up by the crystal-clear purity of the cosmos, by the great starry harmony of the universe.

The disciple of the Buddha longs to enter again into the pure cosmic light and leave the Earth to the darkness. Christ and whoever follows Him goes right through the darkness, in order that one day not only He, but with Him the Earth and the humanity of the Earth can be given back to the cosmic light, to the primordial light. Buddha and the path of Buddha achieves only one part of the great task: it unites with the etheric element and leaves the Earth to the earthly element, to death. Consequently, he does not find the 'I' that can only be found in connection with the earthly element. The etheric element knows only the dissolution into the cosmic element.

Christian metamorphosis

Christ and the path of the imitation of Christ fulfil the whole task. This is not to turn back before the earthly element but to go through it. Through this the earthly element itself is purified and transformed. Not the divesting, but putting on the new garment is emphasised by Paul.* It is the same thought we found in Goethe's *Fairytale*, in the transformation of the broken-apart, wooden hut into the silver altar in the

* [I Cor. 15:53ff.]

Temple. A deep Mystery of highest magic and alchymy[*] is contained in this transformation of the Earth. And on Golgotha the most powerful magic and alchymy of all time has been carried out. With the transformation of the Earth the earthly body of man is itself transformed and renewed. In this lies the Mystery of the resurrection.

The physical is not simply left to death so that the connection with the etheric, living element can then be gained, but in a mysterious manner the physical and the etheric element penetrate each other. Out of the death of the physical element there arises not only an etheric living element, but a new, incorruptible etheric-physical element. Nature places this as in a great picture before us in the transformation of carbon—the basic element of everything organic—into diamond.[†] In the picture of the Holy Grail, we also behold this Mystery. If above we saw what the Grail meant for the 'I', then we see here what it meant for the Earth. In the Holy Grail there lives the renewed earthly element, metamorphosed through the power of the 'I', the physical element that has taken into itself the essence of the etheric, living element, the crystalline element of the cosmos, the carbon that has become again a diamond, the 'Mystery of the philosopher's stone'. In the pictures of the [Grimms'] fairytale *Snow-White*, the glass coffin can be found.[‡] We even found an echo of this with Buddha (above, p. 74 and footnote on p. 74). But there the Mystery was not yet realised in the full sense. Only in Christ could it be so realised, and only in the far future will this transformation and renewal of the Earth be brought to its fulfilment. Only then will the resurrection be real for humanity, as it was for Christ and the disciples on Golgotha.

The path of Buddha does not follow the Christian path in this Mystery of metamorphosis and resurrection. With Buddha we find miracles narrated of the superearthly, spiritual accomplishments of the Perfected One, of *iddhi* and miracles of super-earthly power—with Buddha we find nothing of the 'miracles of the Risen One', of what the disciples experience with the Risen Christ. Buddha's path leads only to *nirvāṇa*, to dissolution in the cosmic ether, not to resurrection and

---

[*] The archaic spelling (Germ. *Alchymie*) seems to be Beckh's attempt to link to the early, true pursuit from later travesties and misunderstandings. See his introduction to the subject in the second book published in *The Mystery of Substance: Alchymy* (forthcoming)—*Tr. note.*

[†] *Cf.* H. B. *Our Origin in the Light*, Germ. ed. 40f.

[‡] 'Snow-White' [Germ. *Die Christengemeinschaft* 1924, Nr. 5. 138–146] in H. B. *Collected Essays and Articles* (forthcoming).

change of the earthly element. Nevertheless, we can learn from Buddha the tremendous thoughts of de-personalisation, of the cosmic experience. Here for us lies the greatness of Buddhism. This super-personal, this cosmic feeling, we then incorporate into that striving which not only reckons with personal destiny, but with the Earth and the future of the Earth. Here is the point where even Buddha, despite all denial of the lower 'I', yet remains personal. The Path which in such a way takes up the Earth and its destiny then leads to resurrection and the transubstantiation of the earthly element. In such a way secrets of ancient Mysteries will become something much more powerful and grandiose, if in the light of Christ they find their renewal.

Initiation in the Sacrament and in the Apocalypse

In such tremendous immensity of the Mysteries, so that it really can take into itself the Earth and the future of the Earth, John the Apocalyptist beholds and presents the path of Christian initiation. How the mystery of the Christian path is in a certain way contained in the Gospels was already known in the Middle Ages. It was recognised how the whole earthly life and suffering of Christ was not only a physical event, but at the same time a picture for what in the depths of the Mysteries was always experienced on the path of initiation in the spiritual-etheric realm. Through the Washing of the Feet, Scourging, Crowning with Thorns, Crucifixion, Burial, all this, it was recognised, now inwardly, spiritually lived through, yet making its effect right into the physical, leads to resurrection.

The Christian stages of suffering on the earlier Christian path that have become the stages of initiation do not find any correspondence in Buddha's path. On this earlier Christian path, the resurrection was still experienced in a certain way in the individual destiny, in such a way that it really takes into itself the whole deed and revelation of Christ and the whole destiny of the Earth. One suffered with it. Thus it is experienced in the Apocalypse of John. This book will be understood in its profundities in the future; the path described there will be followed by an increasing number of people. The Christian path of initiation, the ancient path of initiation of the Mysteries, but in its Christian, in its most Christian future form, is contained in the Apocalypse of John.

The liturgical pictures of the deed at the altar arise out of those depths of the Mysteries where the ancient paths of initiation were followed. In the Christian era this received its Christian form as the 'holy Mass', which today has been newly given to us as the 'Act of Consecration of Man' out of the spiritual world in a form corresponding to the consciousness of our time. The liturgical pictures of the Mass, the deed at the altar, of the conscious deed of human offering, is nothing else but pictures of those degrees of initiation, yet in such a way that they now have taken up the tremendous sacrificial deed of Christ on Golgotha and with this have taken up the essence of Christian initiation. The past and future of the Earth, the past and future of the Mysteries unite in the 'Act of Consecration of Man', of the Mass. And all this lives again in the mysterious pictures of the Apocalypse, the Book of Revelation of John the divine.

The path of Buddha divides into four significant stages (above, p. 55); the ancient initiation of the Mysteries also took place in four significant stages, mirrored in the four stages of the deed at the altar: Gospel, Offertory, Transformation, Communion.

- What we possess in Buddha's path as the first stage of the preparatory moral purification corresponds in the Mass to the Proclamation of the Gospel, connected to the plea for purification (the ancient Mass relates here to Isaiah 6:5–7).
- The actual basis of the Path, meditation, forms the second stage. In the service this becomes the Offertory, the sacrifice of prayer and incense rising up to the divine Ground of the World—of which meditation is definitely the spiritual side: the soul united with Christ prays for the descent of Grace.
- Through this meditation Buddha arrives at the third stage, to the knowledge of earthly suffering.
- This knowledge of suffering leads him to the fourth stage, elimination of the earthly element, to the 'freeing'.

In Christian initiation, the suffering of the earthly element does not remain. Here the earthly element itself is purified and transformed; here it ceases to be suffering. In the place of the third level in Buddha's path, in Christian initiation there appears the metamorphosis and renewal of the Earth itself, which in the Mass appears as metamorphosis, or transubstantiation. And in the place of freeing oneself from the Earth, the fourth level on the Buddha's path, there appears the connection with the transformed and renewed earthly element, the resurrection and communion with the Risen One. In the deed at the altar it corresponds to the 'Communion'.

This fourfold scheme of the Christian path of initiation, at the same time that of the deed at the altar, we find on the tremendous cosmic scale in the Apocalypse of John. We lift ourselves up from the earthly celebration at the altar to the great cosmic celebration at the altar. The whole tremendous process of purification of earthly evolution, as it is presented in the consciousness of the heavenly hierarchies, is experienced and shown by the Apocalyptist in the pictures of the cosmic deed at the altar. The meditation itself into which he enters, the tranquil retreat of the soul, he places before us in the picture on Patmos (Rev. 1:9).

[1] Here he experiences as spiritual beholding, as the great altar picture, the Imagination of Christ the Risen One in the midst of the seven candlesticks. These never fail to be present in this cosmic celebration, as we can spiritually behold with that other tremendous cosmic Deed of Offering forming the beginning of the Bible.* Then there sounds the word of the Gospel, the message to the seven churches, or communities. The book on the altar, whose seal is now opened, contains the Mysteries of earthly evolution, past and future.

[2] We behold in the Lamb the picture of the Offering, as seen from above, from the side of Christ, Who offers Himself to the Earth and to human souls. And in tremendous pictures we are shown how from the censer in the hand of the angel who stands before God (Michael), the smoke of this offering rises up, and how in the smoke the prayers of the saints rise to God. And not only idyllic pictures of super-earthly bliss, as on the Indian Yoga-path of Buddha, are unrolled out of the smoke of this cosmic meditation for the Imaginative consciousness, but all the horrors which are contained in the descent into the abyss of the earthly element rise before the spiritual gaze.

[3] These apocalyptic horrors reach their highest degree with the pouring out of the seven vials of wrath after the sounding of the seven trumpets. Here it goes into the great cosmic transubstantiation, with which as 'God's wrath' everything that obstructs the divine love is excluded in the great process of purifying the earthly element. This cosmic transubstantiation, this change of the earthly element, we feel, cannot proceed without the falling away from the earthly element of that which completely obstructs the divine. And in tremendous words the Apocalyptist speaks of the last censing of the altar preceding the ceremonial act of transformation of the great cosmic sacrificial service (Rev. 15:8):

---

*H. B. *Our Origin in the Light*, Chapter 1, 'Primordial Creation'.

> And the temple was filled with smoke from the glory of God and from his power, and no-one could enter the temple until the seven plagues of the seven angels were completed.

In the pouring out of the seven vials of wrath the tremendous transubstantiation of the Earth takes place. Right through this we are led to the metamorphosis and resurrection of the Earth. And the new, changed Earth descends from above in the picture of the new, the heavenly Jerusalem as the bride in the marriage of the Lamb.

[4] In the 'supper of the Lamb' (Rev. 19:9, 17) we experience the final great act of the cosmic Deed at the altar, the Communion, which here is the communion with the Risen One and the new metamorphosed Earth. What was not yet contained in Buddha's *nirvāṇa,* the renewal and transformed Earth itself first achieved through Golgotha, lies in the picture of the New Jerusalem, the great aim of the future of the Earth itself. The Apocalyptist at the same time places this before us as the aim of the Christian Path.

This Christian Path leads through all the horrors that the Apocalyptist paints in such obscure, tremendous pictures, when it is trodden in complete earnestness through the incarnations. The will, 'Not me and my self-redemption, but the Christ in me and the redemption of the Earth'* can intend nothing other than to want to unite oneself through all these horrors with the destiny of the Earth and all its beings. And in the horrors themselves lies the Mystery of the strength to overcome them. Only right through the horrors does the Path lead to the highest aims, to the holy Temple of the future. This Christian Path of the Apocalyptist that decides to contribute to build the Temple of the future, is no mere initiation into knowledge like the Buddha's Path, but it is an initiation of the will, of the total human being. To the initiation of knowledge, Christ has added for us this initiation of the will. As a testament for the future it rests in the Book of Revelation of the Apocalyptist. And by deciding with our whole person to tread with all our strength this Path of initiation of the will, the soul has taken the decisive step from Buddha to Christ.

---

* Rudolf Steiner, *Christ and the Human Soul,* lecture-course, Norrköping, 12–16 July 1914. GA 155. [A paraphrase of such sayings of Paul as Gal. 2:20—*Tr. addition.*]

Appendix

Steiner and Buddha (Neo-Buddhist Spiritual Streams and Anthroposophy)

At the suggestion of the editor of the *Zeitschrift für Buddhismus* ['Journal for Buddhism'],* while undertaking to write [1931] on this very topical theme, I deliberately choose to deviate from what is otherwise my usual form. For precisely with a presentation of 'Buddhism in the light of Anthroposophy' limited purely to the 'facts', as an anthroposophist and personal student of Rudolf Steiner I would all too easily meet with objections that this 'purely factual' account would somehow be personally coloured, given my personal relationship to Rudolf Steiner and anthroposophy as somewhat tendentious. Consequently, in this case I think it is right to allow everything personally-fated from the outset to feed into my presentation, hoping that just in this way it could succeed to help the reader most honestly in his own judgment to separate the facts from the personal element.

Early studies†

My personally strong inclination towards India and to the Indian spiritual life goes back to earlier years of my life. For many years I was a lawyer before I took up an academic career as a Sanskrit scholar. Then, when starting from the University to enter life and beginning to suffer

* *Zeitschrift für Buddhismus* ['Journal for Buddhism']. This article was not, in fact, ever published. Excerpts are quoted in Gundhild Kačer-Bock's biography of Hermann Beckh. The entire article is published here for the first time. Beckh takes a path unique for one who preferred the impersonal form of address. Here he tells his own story honestly in order to explain, as fully as time allowed him, the anthroposophical contribution to Buddhist studies. Beckh loved the Buddha because he saw his great significance for humanity. The author spoke and wrote in order to share his discoveries. His voice is as contemporary as ever, if not more so today—*Ed. note.*

† Sub-titles added by the Editor.

some things, I felt increasingly drawn to Buddha. I had—and still have today—a very strong personal and spiritual relationship to the great Indian teacher, whom especially through the work of Rudolf Steiner I was allowed to get to know as one of the 'great initiates' of the history of humankind and human development. From the beginning (long before my acquaintance with Rudolf Steiner) I could never see him merely as a 'philosopher' (I never saw him as such) or a proclaimer of intellectual knowledge, a teaching of opinions, but I always felt—and still feel today—him as a being intuitively touched by the cosmic mystery. In short, as an 'esoteric phenomenon' (the same view lies in the Pali word *yakkho* that is used by the Indians for Buddha). For the same reason books on Buddha, like the *Buddhistischer Katechismus* by Subhadra Bhikshu (pen name for '[Friedrich] Zimmerman' [1851-1917])* that I had found earlier on, left me unsatisfied. The noble view on life contained in this book, blissfully lifting one out of the sad everyday niveau (that is expressed in Buddha's words themselves) I could definitely affirm. But to reduce Buddhism, life itself, the whole richness and the abundance of cosmic riddles, to such an intellectual play of questions and answers appeared to me false. Hereby I felt such a disturbing narrowness, whereas I always experienced, and still experience today, from Buddha himself something cosmically wide, something opening the gaze to the widths of the world.

I experienced similar things with Dahlke (whom I also got to know personally in Berlin). I admired and still admire today his intellectual acumen, whereas his dogmatic narrowness, his stubborn dogmatism—like any other dogmatism, not least the Christian one—always repelled me. Today, after his departure, I look at Dahlke as one of those tragic, but in their own way significant, personalities in human history, as a human being from whom I cannot withhold my constant inner sympathy.

With this rejection of the one-sided intellectual neo-Buddhism—whereby I do not want to say that I think all neo-Buddhism from the outset is one-sidedly intellectual—does not approach what has to be said about any kind of 'Theosophical' Buddhism. No representation of Buddhism has repelled me more than that which emerged from the Anglo-Indian Theosophical Movement in the book by Sinnett *Esoteric*

*Subhadra Bhikshu, *Buddhistischer Katechismus*, Leipzig: Max Altmann 1902/ Dresden: Fachbuchverlag 2015; *A Buddhist Catechism*, New York: Putmans 1895/ Marino Fine Books 2013 (reprint of 1920 ed.)/ Forgotten Books 2015, *etc.*

Buddhism [1883]. I found in it neither something esoteric, nor anything from Buddhism, only very much untransformed materialism, passing itself off as 'esoteric'. Only much later did I learn that Rudolf Steiner, too, was very strongly opposed to this book. Also what Annie Besant, who is one-sidedly inclined to Hinduism, says about Buddha and Buddhism did not impress me. On the other hand, I felt a certain spiritual breath in Edwin Arnold's [1832–1904] *The Light of Asia* [1879]. I valued this poetic work provisionally as almost the best thing known to me of Western representations of Buddhist things. In this poem the narration of the youthful experiences of the Bodhisattva particularly appealed to me. It led me in my later Sanskrit period to give special attention to that part of Buddhist literature (*Lalitavistara, etc.*). My own presentation of Buddhism in the 'Göschen Series' (Vol. I, *The Buddha* [1916], p. 28ff.) bears the traces of this work. Subsequent research showed me the way in which cosmic facts are reflected in those 'twelve main events of Buddha's life' the same 'cosmic unity of Twelve' are also expressed in the well-known twelve members (*nidānas*) of the Buddhist series of causal links (*pratītyasamutpāda, paticcasamuppādo*).

Some of the spiritual mood of Buddhism—which I so much missed in Olden's book and in everything which Sanskrit scholars worked on about Buddhism—I found here and there even in the English novelist [Rudyard] Kipling [1865–1936], especially in his amiable book *Kim* [1900] (note the whole character portrayal and final spiritual intuition of Teshoo Lama). The books of [Karl] Gjellerup [1857–1919] (*i.e. The Pilgrim Kamanita* [1906], in which as a Sanskrit scholar I only liked the humorous pastiche of the Indian commentary-style in the robber episode) appeared to me fantastic, too much like a novel. Only the drama *The Wife of the Perfected One* [1907] contained remarkable traits, the episode with Yashodhara (already contained in the Indian Buddha stories) belongs nevertheless to the great dramatic motifs of world literature.

Not that I lacked the organ for the clear thinking of Buddhism, which leads human beings in all higher development to the important 'inner zero-point'. In anthroposophy, too, this 'clarity of thinking' is indeed in the first place valued for everything. I did always very strongly possess the organ for the consecrated and esoteric side of Buddhism precisely in the midst of all simplicity of thought. As the cool breath of the snow-covered mountains relates to the stuffy vapours of large cities and their sultry plains, so I always experienced the clarity and consecration of Buddhist thoughts in the midst of today's decadent and philistine materialism, even of the churches and academic [institutions] (in which through my self-chosen destiny I was involved in such a painful manner).

Wagner

The feeling for this venerable and lofty element of Buddhism I found especially pronounced in Richard Wagner [1813–83], to whom my relationship towards music drew me from my youth onwards, especially after experiencing at a young age [16 years old] a Bayreuth performance of *Parsifal* [1891]. Wagner himself speaks about Buddhism in a remarkable way in his letters to Mathilde Wesendonck. There he once called Buddhism 'a worldview against which most likely any other dogma seems petty and narrow-minded' (letter: Luzern 9 July 1859, p. 161 of the 1st ed.). As firm as this statement of Wagner appears, it does stand beside the fact that Wagner had been led to the presentation of the Christian mystery (in *Parsifal*) through the consequences contained in his life's work of presenting the pre-Christian mysteries (*The Ring* and *Tristan and Isolde*). His life's work culminates in *Parsifal*, his musical-dramatic presentation of the Christian mystery. His intention then still to treat Buddhist material, in the legend of Ananda and Savitri, remained unfulfilled. The fact is that decades before Rudolf Steiner, no one had placed the esoteric side of the Christian mystery, the mysteries of the blood of Golgotha, in such a way before humanity in general as Richard Wagner did. This fact has been recognised in an Easter lecture[*] by Rudolf Steiner himself, who was often critical of Wagner. That this *presenting* of the Christian mystery for Wagner did not mean a glorification of Christian dogma (to which he himself was always averse) should be clear from the whole context of this consideration, in particular from the above-mentioned statement about Buddha. Yet the co-existence of that utterance of Wagner about Buddha and his presentation of the Christian element (not only in *Parsifal*, but already in a certain way in *Tannhäuser*, *Lohengrin*, in *The Mastersingers*)[†] remains significant for everything to be developed in this discussion about the relationship between Steiner and Buddha.

---

[*] The principal lecture seems to be 'Easter: Mystery of the Future'. Berlin, Easter Sunday, April 13, 1908. GA 102—*Ed.*

[†] See H. Beckh, 'Wagner and Christianity' (1933); Eng. tr. in *The Parsifal=-Christ=Mystery*, Leominster: Anastasi, 2015. 11–26—*Tr. note.*

Wagner and Schopenhauer

The *spiritual mood* of Buddhism Wagner had actually laid hold of more intimately than Arthur Schopenhauer [1788–1860], often quoted and deeply revered by him—although Schopenhauer certainly belonged to those who possessed an organ for the spiritual matter of India in general as well as the spiritual essence of Buddhism. He has left us remarkable statements about Buddha.* (Note, for example, his little-noticed reference to the mystery of the name Maya, in *Parerga and Paralipomena,* Vol. II, p. 190, where even the Mercury-mystery associated with Buddha is pointed out: this is an important bridge to certain spiritual-scientific communications of Rudolf Steiner that cannot be gone into in detail on this occasion. So far they have not been observed by any anthroposophist.) This relationship of Wagner to the Buddhist experience is revealed as resting on a certain inner soul-mood, not only in his writings, especially in the previously-mentioned letters to Mathilde Wesendonck. See there, especially what is said on pp. 78 and 105 on the 'Buddhist beggar' and the statement on p. 162: 'I mostly cannot withstand the disgusting impressions of our historical present day in no other way than through a refreshing drink at that sacred spring of the Ganges: one draught from there and everything dwindles to the stature of the activity of ants.'

Yet more deeply and directly than in his words Wagner speaks in his music about everything, about the Mysteries of the world themselves. The innermost esoteric problems of Buddhism are steeped in the dramatic and musical element of the mystery of *Tristan and Isolde.* Nowhere is the 'law of suffering', the suffering of existence, brought to a purely human, so immediately striking, expression, as in the beginning of Act III of *Tristan and Isolde* (think of the 'sad Shepherd's tune' and everything connected with it, especially Tristan's long monologue [III, 1]: 'Must I understand you thus, you ancient, solemn tune....').

***Cf.* the relationship of Schopenhauer to Buddhism in my lecture held at the Dresden Conference of the Schopenhauer Society, 8 June 1927, printed in the 15th *Jahrbuch* of the Schopenhauer Society, 1928 (Heidelberg: Carl Winter), 122–32; Eng. tr. see *Festschrift,* 59–68. The essay also contains many things concerning anthroposophical viewpoints. More on this is contained in my essay 'Rudolf Steiner and the East', in the book *Vom Lebenswerk Rudolf Steiners,* pp. 273–304 [download www.archive.org]; on p. 297 the mystery of the planet Mercury is mentioned. [Eng. tr. in *Hermann Beckh and the Spirit-Word,* Leominster: Anastasi 2015, 33–65; the Mercury-mystery, p. 57f.]

And certainly that which in Buddhism points beyond suffering, properly finds in the music of *Tristan and Isolde* its esoteric expression. Yet seldom has any man written of the mystery of the Buddhist *nirvāṇa* something more satisfying, something that at least is so for me. For these esoteric things, which cannot be expressed in words, can no longer be grasped in thoughts (called *atakkāvacara* in Pali) Wagner has directly found the arguably greatest expression, directly inspired from the world harmony, in the music for *Tristan and Isolde*, not only in the final conclusion, in the final transfiguration of Act III, but already at the beginning of Act II: the extinguishing of the flickering flame, the bright torch of day-consciousness points here to the whole mystery of *saṃsāra* and *nirvāṇa*. In this music mysteries lie, 'which Buddha knew, but for the consciousness of the time could not articulate'.

Buddha's passing

Some of this side of the cosmic-music of the Buddha-mystery I also experienced in many cases in the linguistic side of the Buddhist Pali texts when this for me began to open up through my Indological studies and researches. For the peculiar rhythm and harmony, for the whole of the musical element of the Pali texts I always had an organ. Mostly I found and find this rhythmical-musical element in the grand narrative of the Buddha's passing in the *Mahāparinibbānasutta* in the Dīghanikāya, which belongs to the most important and valuable Buddhist texts. As a human document of the first order, this *Mahāparinibbānasutta* has a meaning far beyond Buddhism, old and new. The revelation of mankind in the personality of the great initiate contained therein can be perceived—as I understand the word—as something directly Christian.

For everything which I have experienced on the above-mentioned Buddhist text that for decades was an inner companion for me, especially, too, what I experienced of the rhythmical Pali text, my translation of *Der Hingang des Vollendeten*, published by Die Christengemeinschaft (Stuttgart 1925; Eng. tr. *The Passing of the Perfect One*, forthcoming) was to convey an idea. Many words and phrases were inwardly wrestled with for years, for decades. That is, one cannot outwardly force such translations. You have to wait until they slowly fashion themselves from within. The musical-rhythmical element was sought for in the third and fourth, and mostly in the fifth chapter, worked out in the episode under the Sala trees right into the choice of vowels and consonants. As Wagner expresses the esoteric element of Buddhism in musical expression, I was looking to recoup this musical element in the element of speech. To bring out in German, or any Western language, the perfect musical element of the Pali text will never be possible. In any case, I was striving to give at least a faint idea of what hovered as an ideal translation. For the popular translations of Buddha's words, be it by Francke, or Neumann (to mention two very different examples) could never really satisfy me. Also, it lay close to my heart after giving up my academic profession through this translation published by The Christian Community to retain a certain inner connection with my former professional work. My work on Buddhism (*Buddha's Life and Teaching*) published in the 'Göschen Series' in two volumes arose at a time when I was still in the academic profession, but already a student of Rudolf Steiner. But nothing immediately flowed out of anthroposophy into this publication. The book contained nothing that cannot be directly verified and documented from the Buddhist texts. But there are many things in these texts, which touch on anthroposophy and anthroposophic meditation, though anthroposophy and Buddhism are very different in their nature.

But with that which I would like to call the musical element in the *Passing of the Perfected One*, with my translation of the Buddhist *Mahāparinibbānasutta*, I was influenced by a passage in Rudolf Steiner on the basic lines of anthroposophic meditation practice developed in the book *Knowledge of the Higher Worlds* [GA 10], which (it is already mentioned as the end of my introduction for my *Buddha's Passing*) I would like to quote once more. Rudolf Steiner mentions the effect of certain exercises on the inner soul-organism. Steiner says:[*]

> At this point the spiritual world is entered. If the student has advanced so far, he acquires a new understanding for all that the great teachers of mankind have uttered. The sayings of the Buddha and the gospels, for instance produce a new effect on him. They pervade him with a rapture of which he had not dreamed before. For the tone of their words follows the movements and rhythms which he has himself formed within himself. He can now have positive knowledge that a Buddha or the evangelists did not utter their own revelation but those which flowed into them from the inmost being of things. A fact here must be pointed out which can only be understood in the light of what has been said above. The many repetitions

[*]GA 10, tr. Metaxa, rev. Monges. New York: Anthroposophic Press 1947, 3rd ed., 170f.

> in the sayings of the Buddha are not comprehensible to people of our present evolutionary stage. For the esoteric student, however, they become a force on which he gladly lets his inner senses rest, for they correspond with certain movements in the etheric body. Devotional surrender to them, with perfect inner peace, creates an inner harmony with these movements; and because the latter are an image of certain cosmic rhythms which also at certain points repeat themselves and revert to former modes, the student listening to the wisdom of the Buddha unites his life with that of the context of the cosmic mysteries.

Such statements on the Buddha can be found in Rudolf Steiner, although he never stood for Buddhism as a religion of the present (he never stood for any 'religion', for any dogmatic knowledge). He rather rejected all passing trends. The quoted passage has always given me a lasting impression influencing much of my work.

Buddha's teaching of meditation

Especially on the points mentioned here my discussion of Buddha and his teaching appears fruitful. With the path of knowledge and meditation the theme 'Anthroposophy and Buddhism' becomes especially serious in a practical manner. What is the decisive greatness and everlasting greatness of Buddha? The fact that he was no mere 'philosopher', no ordinary 'religious founder' but the *teacher* ('esoteric teacher') of the *path of meditation and knowledge,* and that he placed openly before the world the path of meditation, which until then had been practiced in closed Yoga groups. Buddha himself emphasised the primary importance of this path in as much as the 'Sermon of Benares' first proclaimed it (the noble 'Eightfold Path') and only then the simple truth of suffering, which in the fourth of its stages again includes the 'Eightfold Path'. That is and remains a fact of human and world significance. But why—one could ask—do we still need Rudolf Steiner and *Knowledge of the Higher Worlds*? Not only the fact *that* Buddha has placed in the open the path for humanity, the path of spiritual practice, of meditation, but also the scheme of the Eightfold Path scheme itself requires a certain universal significance for humanity. Rudolf Steiner also recognised this fact in the way he worked the scheme of the Eightfold Path with a specific reference in his presentation of the path of knowledge, although the many other things in this presentation are not all exhausted in the scheme of the Eightfold Path.

This means the universal significance of the Eightfold Path is not contested in anthroposophy, but of course this Eightfold Path opens the question: what *is* right view, right resolve, what *is* right speech, right action, what *is* consciousness, what *is* right meditation? Especially in the schematic vagueness of the formula lies something of its universal validity, of its adaptability to all kinds of temporal relations and human conditions. Now it is not as if even Buddha would have given a clear answer to all the questions mentioned. This answer cannot be found in the scheme of the Path itself, but in entirely different contexts. A main textual source of this is the *Sāmaññaphalasutta* of the Dīghanikāya, one of the most important, most valuable and most interesting texts of world literature. The description contained therein of the path of meditation is then passed over into a number of other texts of the Dīghanikāya. On this account my presentation of the Buddhist path is essentially based on the second little volume of my Göschen book (p. 22ff.), and in its four main parts:

> *sīla* (moral self-discipline, right ethical behaviour),
> *samādhi* (meditation),
> *paññā* (knowledge),
> *vimutti* (liberation).

The meditation chapter (p. 38ff.) is practically the most important and interesting. Nobody has pointed, as Buddha has, so openly and forcefully and with such detail to the crucial practical importance of meditation practice and has reached such wide groups with his proclamation. But in all these concrete instructions on meditation, Buddhism touches throughout on Indian Yoga. To question this connection of the practice of Buddhist meditation with Indian Yoga, which I have justified and illuminated in my writings on Buddha, has no meaning. (Göschen *Buddha*, Vol. I, p. 121ff.; Vol. 2, p. 10ff., 38ff.) Even though the mere outer aspect of *āsana* and *prāṇāyama* withdraws in Buddhist meditation practice (on the relationship of Buddha to the mystery of breathing of Yoga, see Vol. 2, p. 41), the whole of this exercise is nevertheless carried throughout by the spirit of Yoga. And therein lies also the reason why this exercise is technically unfeasible under the current cultural conditions. This is true even, or even primarily, of this first main part of this exercise: the fulfilment of the ethical requirements, *i.e.* the realisation of the ideal of the Indian holy man (which was also entirely demanded by Buddha) up to the last consequences. This ideal cannot be fulfilled under the current cultural situation, not only because of the weakness of the individual, but also because of the conditions and limits set for individual by the world of which he is a part.

Any teaching to agree intellectually with any of Buddha's teaching, or even the intellectual teaching of Yoga, to give oneself intellectually or even with one's heart, to confess it, is easy and simple. Someone seriously attempting to realise it practically will be faced with the experience that he cannot achieve the meditation exercise and the realisation of its stages sought on Indian paths. In full recognition of the human values and the values for the future that are contained in the 'Path' itself and the scheme of the Eightfold Path, he finds on the closer instruction concerning the realisation of the values contained in the Eightfold scheme: as a Westerner such can no longer be found on the Indian path today. In this situation described here, I found myself when I met Rudolf Steiner and the book *Knowledge of the Higher Worlds: How is it Attained?* Both showed a way to achieve what could not be achieved on the Indian path that was ardently sought and striven for after so long.

In this whole contemplation little has been mentioned on the question of 'Buddha and Christ', 'Steiner and Christ', and here the point is reached where it needs to be addressed in more detail. For where the human being stands at the inner zero-point, which was described in the previous section—and none of the great teachers of humanity has purely disclosed this 'zero-point' more clearly and openly than Buddha (I shall return to this question later), so also he stands consciously or unconsciously before the decisive encounter with Christ in his life, as the most serious of all life's tests. But at this point an entire heap of childish religious prejudices have first be cleared away, if what one wants to say from the heart is to be understood.

Early encounters and the zero-point

With what I experienced in church and religion lessons concerning Christ, already as a child I could never make anything of importance. In later years many things could only alienate me and made me suspicious of Christianity. In the sultriness of the everyday it did not help me to breathe, whereas in Indian things I could always experience the cool and refreshing breath of the 'fields of snow of the Himalayas'. Not through tradition and ecclesiastical contexts, but simply through life's destiny, through *karma,* as they say in India, did Christianity reach me. I saw myself placed before the experience, or one day knew at least intuitively, that esoteric facts are contained in Indian, Iranian and Egyptian traditions, as also in the Bible, in the Old and New Testaments, not least in the Gospels—think, for example, of Christ's healing the sick. In these esoteric facts there appeared to me the 'meaning of life'.

The first strong Christian impression of my life was the above-mentioned performance of *Parsifal* in Bayreuth [1891]. I was then 16 years old. What I call here an inner 'Christ encounter' became a fully conscious experience only during the time of my acquaintance with Rudolf Steiner, but already then was laid as a seed. The basis was then already laid for everything that later led me to anthroposophy. In my *The Parsifal-Christ-Experience in Wagner's Music Drama* (Stuttgart: Die Christengemeinschaft 1930; Eng. tr. Leominster: Anastasi 2015), which was written only in the spring of last year [1930], it is clearly stated what I understand with 'Christ encounter'. I believe that just this writing justifies my use of this term with the hope of being understood. For with the word 'Christ' much can be misused. But the above-mentioned writing can lead to an 'experience of Christ'; this can rest for a long time in the subconscious, how it is initially experienced in sleep and how led by certain destinies it gradually comes ever more clearly into consciousness. Finally, by undergoing diverse trials, it can become a fully conscious soul-experience. Even the word 'Grail quest' can be applied to the category of soul-experiences referred to here. Certain childhood experiences—in later times, all things being equal, I had often to think of Buddha's childhood experience under the rose-apple tree—through the Bayreuth-experience became ever more conscious. The Grail imagination was actually always the highest and most decisive, an important point that I always sought in vain in the Indian spiritual world. I could not find it there.* Through meeting Rudolf Steiner also in this regard many only subconscious or semiconscious things were brought into the full light of consciousness.

The described experiences, especially, too, those of the Christian Gospel, in connection with my whole attitude to Eastern spiritual life

*This, as I now see things, is only partly true. Besides the Christian Imagination of the Holy Grail—as the chalice of the Blood of Golgotha—there is a pre-Christian one that also shines into the Buddha legend (the chalice made of beryl), in which cosmic nourishment was offered to the Buddha child in his mother's womb (Göschen *Buddha*, II, 32).

(which gradually for my outer professional destiny also became increasingly decisive) made me think early on about the important question of 'Buddha and Christ'. At the University of Berlin I held provisional lectures on the questions stimulated first by Seydel and van den Berg ('The Relationship of the Christian gospels particularly the gospel of Luke, to Buddhist sources'). For someone who not only as philologist but as an esotericist approaches the problems, there arises early on the concept of 'the initiate' as the human being who has advanced in esoteric experience. Nothing is more obvious but to ask oneself: Well, there are those who are well advanced in esoteric experience, these are the 'great initiates' of humanity. Even Buddhism itself speaks, as is known, of a plurality of the great initiates of humanity, such as Krishna, Zarathustra, Buddha. Such were 'great initiates'—and besides them others, albeit in a manifold gradation of initiation degrees—thus one will ask oneself: Would Jesus of Nazareth—the Christ-Jesus, as he is called by his followers—have been such an 'initiate'? There comes naturally to the elementary esoteric-seeking beginner to attempt a solution of the Christ-question on the path of thinking outlined here. This attempt seemed to me obvious. But time and again I came in its implementation on an obscure difficulty. The figure of Christ of the Gospels did not want to be so easily classified into the conceptual category of initiates, of the great adepts of mankind. On the one hand, He appeared less than such an 'initiate' (because more human, more accessible to human feelings and sufferings, more removed from the concept of the 'superman' of the great initiates, as is attributed by the Indians to the Buddha). On the other hand more unique, incomparable, divine. A 'residue' not to be expressed in words, not to be grasped in thinking, appeared to remain over in such attempts at thought.

Here, too, I reached a 'zero-point' of thinking and questioning, until in meeting Rudolf Steiner, the unique, outstanding and decisive Christ-proclaimer in our time, the answer became clear. The answer made many things understandable. The previous attempts to solve it were inadequate, leading to no real solution. Basically, with this experience of one's own inner inability, it has to do with the same inner zero-point, as earlier described. In both cases (with the question of meditation) the answer came from the side of Christ, after Buddha had led me to the zero-point. And it doesn't mean an easy and convenient answer, but an answer for which inwardly I had to wrestle, really developed by the ego.

The lost human archetype regained

I am consequently unsure whether and to what extent it is here possible to bring some of that answer to the understanding of the wider public, but I will try to the extent that it seems necessary for the subject of this consideration, 'Steiner and Buddha'. In order to lead to the question of Christ, Steiner leads the gaze initially towards the Jesus-child, especially in the infancy narrative of Luke's Gospel. Therein that divine childlike being felt revealed, which was also revealed in Krishna, so deeply inspiring the Indian culture. Also that 'rays (rays of love) of the Buddha'—the Indologist should take certain north-Buddhist imaginations to his aid in order to follow with his understanding—were involved in the event of Bethlehem. Here initially only the bodily sheaths were fashioned for the later entrance of the Christ-Being, taking place at the Jordan-baptism. When Jesus of Nazareth grew into manhood and stood with John the Baptist at the Jordan, there lived in him as a result of the weaving of destiny, which I cannot describe in detail now, a revelation of Zoroaster (the first, primal Zarathustra, who is mentioned in Plutarch). There he carried in himself an embodiment of the great human initiate, at this moment was himself a great initiate. The wise one, the carrier of highest human wisdom, connected himself with the 'divine child'. Neither that divine child, nor this high, but human, wise one is in their own being the Christ, although Christ from the beginning oversaw the whole unique becoming of that Jesus-being. Only through this could the cosmic Christ entity, the solar Logos, the Sun-'I' (in which the higher human ego and the divine human prototype lived) be revealed in the bodily sheath of Jesus of Nazareth, that this bodily sheath was relinquished from the 'I' of the great initiate of humanity, that the highest human ego through its self-sacrifice makes room for the divine 'I'. Roughly, as far as human words can express something like this, the Jordan-event is portrayed by Rudolf Steiner as the Incarnation of Christ. From then on, Christ was no longer an 'initiate' as it is normally understood, but simply 'the revelation of humanity'. The lost human archetype was again present in Him; the divinity itself in Him took part in everything human, including the sufferings of humanity, experienced even in the human body our human fate of death.

Only three years, Rudolf Steiner said—or about as long as a child in the first age is directly connected with the higher spiritual beings—could the divine Christ-being live in the earthly bodily sheath. Then through world-karma circumstances had to be such as to release this connection. In the experience of the blood of Golgotha the divine, heavenly light-substance re-connects with the darkened Earth; the Earth itself then becomes the 'body of Christ', with whose elevation she matures towards a new level of existence. And as before through the darkening of the earthly element for the human being, his true higher Self was also obscured—consequently Buddha had to leave for the people this Higher Self (*ātman*) in an indeterminate state, as it were in the vanishing point of the irrational, because the human being in the practical outcome of this had lost this 'I'—so now, through all that the Christ-sacrifice meant for the Earth, the Self could also light up in the human being again when he seeks to connect to the Christ-'I'. With all this Rudolf Steiner touches on the Mystery of the Holy Grail, places the innermost sense of the Grail-experience before humanity. And I now experience like a guiding of destiny how I was prepared internally by the *Parsifal*-experience in Bayreuth for Steiner's message of Christ.

Buddha, the Gospel and the Maitreya Buddha

As is clear from the above, Rudolf Steiner also fully acknowledging the concept 'initiate', fully admits the fact that the human initiate exists. The exceeding greatness and significance of the initiate Buddha—whose rays of love even shine into the Christmas night of the Gospel—is always expressly emphasised by him. From ever-changing, ever-fresh esoteric viewpoints the greatness of the initiate Buddha is illuminated by Rudolf Steiner, pointing to the meaning of the 'experience under the sacred fig tree'. There existed *before* Christ, before the turning point of time, such initiated Buddhas, as they are called in Buddhism, and there will also be such in the future, in the Christian era of humankind. The Maitreya Buddha, to which the Buddhist tradition points to as the Buddha of the future, and should not be confused with Christ Himself, will be the next of these great initiates. The proclamation of Christ in his teaching will play a decisive role. (He will be one of the great proclaimers of the Christ-Event.) *But the Christ event itself*, the Mystery of Golgotha, as Rudolf Steiner always calls it, *is something unique in world-history*, is as it were the fulcrum of the scales* of the

*The image here is of the old-fashioned scales consisting of two pans suspended from a balancing point, the fulcrum. The part played by the zodiacal Scales in the Gospel story is explained in detail in Beckh's expositions of the Gospels of Mark and John—*Tr. note.*

Earth, the central event touching everything past and everything in the future destiny of the Earth. The proclamation of all the initiates still to come, of the Buddha Maitreya himself, will gain through this Christ-Event a different, a new character and content. Mysteries which the last revealed Buddha could not reveal, because the Earth and mankind was not yet ripe to perceive it, will then be able to be revealed.

Buddha himself stresses with the greatest emphasis, how he cannot disclose to humanity everything he knows. We are to be repeatedly reminded of the episode in the Simsapā-forest (Samyuttanikāya, V, p. 437): Buddha in the presence of the disciples takes some Simsapā leaves into his hands, explaining: like the few leaves in his hands compared to the many leaves in Simsapā-forest, so is the ratio of the few things that he has communicated in his teachings to the many which he knows and has not shared (Göschen *Buddha*, Vol. I, p. 110). In assessing a purely spiritual phenomenon, as in the early, pre-Christian times of Buddha, and in the completely altered cultural conditions today, as for Rudolf Steiner, one might easily be confused. One has to see how the interaction of such a teacher of humanity, in a way that is incomprehensible to the abstract scholar of today, indeed perhaps offensive, is a strictly *educational* one. (Buddha himself, in the sacred texts themselves, is called 'an incomparable educator who reins in the human herd'.) Each word that such a teacher speaks is strictly measured according to these great human, educational criteria. Moreover, humanity's educational tasks at different times and under different cultural conditions are very diverse.

Rudolf Steiner always emphatically stressed that the change and development of the consciousness of humanity plays a crucial role. The initiate Zarathustra has prophetically foretold the Christ-event and pointed out its importance (see the prophecy of Christ in the Avesta cited in the original text and in translation at the end of my little book *Zarathustra*). Even Buddha would have known about this Mystery, but under the existing cultural conditions, 500 years before Golgotha, there was no possibility to communicate it to people. His own work, as Steiner shows, does stand in a certain relation to that Event. The solar rays of Christ were then already beginning to draw near to the Earth. The parabolic sayings of the Buddha, who always refers to the appearance of the rising of the Sun shining above the Morning Star as a particularly high revelation of spiritual light, receive there a profound meaning for many today as yet unsuspected...

Because in Christ and in the Christ-Event itself lies the meaning of the Earth, everything changes its name in the light of this Event. A great initiate such as Buddha—again emphatically emphasised by Steiner—always speaks the truth. This is also true for the 'knowledge from suffering' proclaimed by Buddha. But the fact rightly recognised by Buddha, that all the suffering associated with the Earth and not penetrated by Christ—is gradually being removed by Christ's Being. He is increasingly penetrating the Earth and human souls. 'Why could Christ work effectively?', asks Steiner in the Düsseldorf lecture-cycle,* and he gives the answer: 'Because Buddha has spoken the truth.' No other saying than this can so clearly disclose Rudolf Steiner's fundamental attitude toward Buddha.

Further questions

The earthly element itself, about which the great initiate Buddha has left for us correct statements and judgments, changes its meaning and its essence with the event of Golgotha. In the light of this statement or proclamation of Rudolf Steiner, I want to point as a conclusion to a point appearing important to me, concerning which Steiner has never spoken about himself. Unfortunately I missed the opportunity, during a time when such things were still possible, to ask him concerning this. The fact to which I refer is that of what is called the north, or Mahayana Buddhism, which from the turning point of time onwards, gained an ever greater following as the original Buddhism increasingly receded in India. In connection with the discourse of Buddha with Ananda, his teaching, under certain conditions that are now occurring (it had to do with admitting women to the spiritual paths) would only exist for 500 years. Either Buddha would have been wrong with this statement, then he would not have been an initiate, or we would have to say what persisted after 500 years as Buddhism still existing as such within Buddha's conception is no longer the original, the true and pure teaching. Just the fact that Buddha here speaks of 500 years, that is, the period lying between Buddhism and the turning point of time (in Steiner's view as well as our whole Christian calculation of time), causes one to think.

The question arises for someone who has gained a relationship to Rudolf Steiner's world-conception: should it be a coincidence that the

* Rudolf Steiner, *The Spiritual Hierarchies and their Reflection in the Physical World*. Düsseldorf, 12 Jan. 1909. GA 110.

moment of time given by Buddha indicated for the ending of his teaching originally proclaimed by him *leads to the Christ Event*? Should Buddha himself have believed that through the said Event, the truth of the recommendations issued by him is not contradicted, but in the way Steiner, too, means, certain actual conditions of that proclamation (of the truth of suffering) would have been removed? Does not the simple historical fact exist that Buddhism itself, as the original Buddhism in India declined, from this moment on, it increasingly spreads in a modified form as northern Buddhism (the Mahayana system) in Asia? Does there not lie in the basic idea of Mahayana—in which the effect is not only for one's own salvation, but for the salvation of the world, for all mankind*—already a Christian viewpoint of view, not in the sense of organised Christianity, but in the sense in which Steiner understands Christianity?

Steiner repeatedly explained how even in the West today the Christ-Impulse is only in the very first, faint beginnings of its realisation. One cannot possibly say that Mahayana Buddhism is that form in which the Christ-Impulse in a certain way first penetrated in the East. In this case it does not depend (as is the case today already in a certain way in India) that if one somehow deliberately looks at the Christ-Event in the East, that Christian teaching would have consciously been taken up. A deliberate looking to the Mystery of Golgotha in Mahayana Buddhism certainly does *not* exist, though certain legends of Buddha's self-sacrifice in previous incarnations contain echoes of it. But, as Steiner always thought, the Christ-event acts on human souls, still not understanding; it is nevertheless at work objectively out of the earthly contexts, acting on the whole of earthly happenings and human affairs. *The simple fact that the Christ has now connected Himself to the Earth and humanity*. Thus 500 years before the Christian era in the East, the impulse of mankind received another character. The whole fact of Mahayana Buddhism—but, as I said, this is only my personal hypothesis, not a point of view on which Steiner himself would have placed a value—could in this sense, be used as a testimony for the effect Steiner reports for the Earth's history and for human history of the Christ-Event.

And at the same time with this a viewpoint would be given for one who has found in Rudolf Steiner's 'anthroposophy' the decisive key to

* 'Not I and my own redemption, but Christ in me and the redemption of the Earth', is a freely rendered saying by Steiner, following Paul [Gal. 2:20].

the solution of the present tasks, the concern with the question of the Buddha, making it a permanently important and significant task for recognition. Steiner himself—this was emphasised here—has repeatedly returned to these questions of the Buddha in his teaching that has illuminated the greatness and importance for humanity of the initiate Buddha from ever new viewpoints. Only the least of these spiritual-scientific communications by Steiner about Buddha could be provisionally mentioned here. So we could not yet discuss today the important theme of reincarnation:* 'How does the anthroposophic knowledge of reincarnation relate to the Indian and Indian-Buddhist teaching of reincarnation and the teaching of salvation?' It appeared initially important to unfold the whole question of 'Steiner and Buddha' in an appropriate form for a non-anthroposophic audience, giving the necessary basis—including a personal connection—for a possible subsequent detailed discussion of these things.

Rudolf Steiner has never suggested Buddhism as a dogma for the present-day. He also never wanted anthroposophy to be understood as a dogma, but always as a path of knowledge—'a path of knowledge, that would lead the spiritual in the human being to the spiritual in the universe'. But in terms of wrestling with the questions of knowledge as given [us] by Buddha, in terms of showing human values, which for the present and for the future are still contained in the teaching of Buddha, a stream is represented in this journal and also still possible for the anthroposophic thinker even today. Indeed, the author of these observations could imagine many reasons that especially today would be fruitful, and contribute to establish today a nobler view of the world and of life to be shared further afield. This could also prepare the ground for the emergence one day of a higher Christianity than the one hitherto. For the anthroposophist, Buddha, too, is an important forerunner of Christ. And he does not believe that the great, pre-Christian Mystery impulses would be finished through Christianity, but that especially through the Christ-Event and in the light of Christ in the

*Grimm, in his book *Die Lehre des Buddha,* rightly misses the concept of reincarnation in the dogma of the Christian church. This can be answered with the Christian worldview brought in a contemporary manner by anthroposophy. This contains in particular the concept of repeated earthly lives. It also shows on the one hand how this knowledge receives its full meaning especially in the light of the Christ-Event, and how on the other hand the Christian Impulse gains its full future-carrying meaning in the light of this knowledge, which has probably been expressed for the first time in history in early India.

future they would receive a new and heightened significance, re-appearing on a higher Christian (or 'I') level. In my book *John's Gospel: The Cosmic Rhythm – Stars and Stones* we find this idea elaborated with regard to John 4 (Christ and the Samaritan woman at the well).

Buddhism, as has been said here, is not a philosophy, but an impulse of humanity, a path of knowledge—a path of meditation. As such, however, it can itself become again an object of philosophic reflection; as we know, it already became such in early India. In particular the important and interesting Madhyamika philosophy has to be mentioned here. Again, important and rewarding tasks remain for a modern neo-Buddhist movement, though the questions discussed here hardly arise. Important and meaningful is the Vedantic monistic doctrine; in many respects the dualistic teaching of the Sankhya and Yoga philosophy is richly suggestive. The Indians had and would allow the co-existence of many only apparently contradictory systems of thought. Steiner also emphasises that there are many possible ideological considerations; he speaks again significantly about 7 × 12 possible world-views, arriving at a number (84) which is a sacred number in Buddhism.

The monist teaching of the Vedanta, which besides its unquestionable content of truth, its greatness and sublimity, also contains the danger of a certain superficiality, of decaying into a situation of empty abstraction and tautologies in eternal repetition of the same. Compared with this the Buddhist teachings appear as the 'philosophy of zero-time and the zero point'—at the beginning of the series of numbers there does not stand unity, but zero. The Buddhist teachings—as it were, the still uneven all-important and deeper, 'more esoteric' conception of the world, appear as the actual crowning of Indian thought, in the same way as the Buddhist path of meditation was the crowning of Indian Yoga.

To expound on this on the path of philosophical thinking in detail would be a praiseworthy task for the neo-Buddhist. For its fulfilment, it would be desirable [to include], besides the knowledge of Buddhist philosophy, also the knowledge of anthroposophy—which in this realm has much to offer—combined with a mastery of advanced mathematics and that brilliant eye for esoteric-spiritual mathematics that, for example, Novalis possessed for it. At the end of this contribution certain important paths of contemporary Buddhist research may be gently suggested.

The Works of Prof. Hermann Beckh
Dr jur. et phil.

'An abundance of books came into existence whose significance perhaps will only be properly appreciated in the future.'
(Lic. Emil Bock, 'Hermann Beckh' in *Zeitgenossen Weggenossen Wegbereiter*, Stuttgart: Urachhaus 1959. 132)

*

Die Beweislast nach dem Bürgerlichen Gesetzbuch
'The Burden of Proof according to the Code of Civil Law'
Prize essay, awarded distinction from the Law Faculty the University of Munich
München and Berlin 1899. Download: http://dlib-pr.mpier.mpg.de/m/kleioc/0010/exec/books/%22103926%22/

Ein Beitrag zur Textkritik an Kālidāsas Meghadūta
'A contribution for the text criticism of Kālidāsa's Meghadūta'
Doctorate dissertation approved by the Department of Philosophy of the University of Berlin 1907.

Die tibetische Übersetzung von Kālidāsas Meghadūta
'The Tibetan translation of Kālidāsa's Meghadūta'
Edited and with a German translation, Berlin 1907/2011.

Beiträge zur tibetischen Grammatik, Lexikogaphie, Stilistik und Metrik
Habilitationsschrift. Berlin 1908.
'Contributions to Tibetan grammar, lexicography, style and prosody'
Inaugural dissertation.

Udānavarga
A collection of Buddhist sayings in the Tibetan language.
Berlin 1911 (also reprinted by Walter de Gruyter, 2013).

Verzeichnis der tibetischen Handschriften
'Catalogue of Tibetan MSS in the Royal Library in Berlin' (Vol. 24 of the Manuscript Catalogue). First division: Kanjur (Bhak-Khgur).
Berlin 1914/2011/14.

Buddha und seine Lehre
'Buddha and his Teaching.' Vol. 1: The Life. Vol. 2: The Teaching.
Sammlung Göschen. Berlin & Leipzig 1916. Third edition 1928.
Later one-volume editions, Stuttgart: Urachhaus 1958/1998/2012.
Tr. into Dutch and Japanese.
Eng. tr. *Buddha's Life and Teaching* (forthcoming).

'Rudolf Steiner und das Morgenland'
in *Vom Lebenswerk Rudolf Steiners*
Ed. Friedrich Rittelmeyer, München: Chr. Kaiser 1921
Reprint by HP, Univ. of Michigan (www.lib.umich.edu) (download: www.archive.org).
Eng. tr. in *Hermann Beckh and the Spirit-Word,* Leominster: Anastasi 2015. 33–65.

[1] *Der physische und der geistige Ursprung der Sprache*
The physical and the spiritual origin of language. Stuttgart 1921.
[2] *'Es werde Licht!'*
'Let there be light!'
The primal biblical words of creation and the primal significance of the sounds in the light of spiritual science. Stuttgart 1921.
[3] *Etymologie und Lautbedeutung*
Etymology and the significance of speech sounds in the light of spiritual science.
Stuttgart 1922/2013.
These three essays on language reprinted in:
Neue Wege zur Ursprache, Stuttgart 1954
Eng. tr. *New Ways to the Source of Speech,* includes two extra essays 'Indology and Spiritual Science' (forthcoming).

Anthroposophie und Universitätswissenschaft
'Anthroposophy and University Knowledge'
Breslau 1922. Eng. tr. in *Hermann Beckh and the Spirit-Word,* Leominster: Anastasi 2015. 71–101.

Vom geistigen Wesen der Tonarten
With diagrams. Breslau 1922. Third edition 1932.
Eng. tr. *The Essence of Tonality: An Attempt to view musical Problems in the Light of Spiritual Science.* Leominster: Anastasi 2008.

Der Ursprung im Lichte
Stuttgart 1924
Eng. tr. *Our Origin in the Light: Pictures from Genesis* (forthcoming).

Von Buddha zu Christus
Stuttgart 1925 (tr. in Norwegian, Oslo 1926);
Eng. tr. *From Buddha to Christ* selections 1978; Eng. tr. of complete text with 'Steiner and Buddha' (article from a lecture, 1931) Temple Lodge Publishing 2019.

Das neue Jerusalem / 'The New Jerusalem'
A poetic work, in the collaborative work *Gegenwartsrätsel im Offenbarungslicht* ('Problems of the present in the light of revelation'), Stuttgart 1925.

Eng. tr. incl. in *John's Gospel: The Cosmic Rhythm – Stars and Stones*. Leominster: Anastasi 2015.

Der Hingang des Vollendeten
Stuttgart 1925/60.
Eng. tr. with Introduction: *The Passing of the Perfect One and his Nirvāṇa (Mahāparinibbāna-Sutta of the Pali Canon* (forthcoming).

Zarathustra
Stuttgart 1927
Eng. tr. in *From the Mysteries* (forthcoming double volume).

Aus der Welt der Mysterien
Basel 1927;
Eng. tr. *From the World of the Mysteries,* Seven articles (reprinted) with *Zarathustra* (forthcoming).

Der kosmische Rhythmus im Markus-Evangelium
Basel 1928/60/97.
Eng. tr. *Mark's Gospel: The Cosmic Rhythm,* Leominster: Anastasi 2015.

Der kosmische Rhythmus, das Sternengeheimnis und Erdengeheimnis im Johannes-Evangelium
Basel 1930.
Eng. tr. *John's Gospel: The Cosmic Rhythm – Stars and Stones,* Leominster: Anastasi 2015.

Das Christus-Erlebnis im Dramatisch-Musikalischen von Richard Wagners 'Parsifal'
Stuttgart 1930.
Eng. tr. *The Parsifal=Christ=Experience in Wagner's Music Drama*
with H. B. 'Richard Wagner and Christianity' (1933), also essays by Emil Bock (1928) and Rudolf Frieling (1956), Leominster: Anastasi 2015.

Vom Geheimnis der Stoffeswelt (Alchymie)
Basel 1931/37/42/2007/13
Eng. tr. *The Mystery of the Material World: Alchemy* (forthcoming).

Der Hymnus an die Erde
Germ tr. and commentary. Stuttgart 1934/60.
Eng. tr. *The Hymn to the Earth: From the Old Indian Atharvaveda*: A memorial to the oldest poem and to the early Aryans (forthcoming).

Psalm 23 aus der Heiligen Schrift
Newly translated from the original text and set to music, op. 7.
Stuttgart 1935.

Die Rosen von Damaskus
The Roses of Damascus. 'Thibaut von Champagne'. The ballad by Conrad

Ferdinand Meyer. For solo high voice with piano accompaniment set to music, op. 8. Stuttgart 1937.

Die Sprache der Tonart
Stuttgart 1937/87/99
Eng. tr. *The Language of Tonality in the Music from Bach to Bruckner with special reference to Wagner's Music Dramas,* Leominster: Anastasi 2015.
Richard Wagner und das Christentum
Richard Wagner and Christianity
Stuttgart 1933. Eng. tr. incl. in *The Parsifal=Christ=Experience in Wagner's Music Drama.* Leominster: Anastasi 2015.

Indische Weisheit und Christentum
Stuttgart 1938.
Eng. tr. *Indian Wisdom and Christianity*
A collection of articles, 10 reprinted and 9 from the literary estate, also incl. in *Collected essays and Articles* (forthcoming).

Das Geheimnis des musikalischen Schaffens: Der Mensch und die Musik
A recently discovered history of music in Ms:
Five chapters pub. in three articles in *Der Europäer,* Basel 09.2005/09.2006/02.2007–08:
http://www.perseus.ch/archive/category/europaer/europaer-archiv
Eng. tr. *The Mystery of Musial Creativity: The Human Being and Music* (forthcoming).

Collected Essays and Articles
Over 80 items on Eastern religion, Yoga, Christianity, 'Snow-White', language, *etc.*
www.rudolf-steiner-bibliothek.de holds an almost complete collection of the original journals).

Biography:
Gundhild Kačer-Bock (d. 2008), *Hermann Beckh: Leben und Werk*
Stuttgart 1997.
Eng. tr. *Hermann Beckh: Life and Work,* Leominster: Anastasi 2016.

Hermann Beckh and the Spirit-Word: Orientalist, Christian Priest and Independent Scholar
Leominster: Anastasi 2015.
Includes:
A. S. 'Hermann Beckh and the Twenty-First Century'
H. B. 'Rudolf Steiner and the East'
H. B. 'Anthroposophy and University Knowledge'
H. B. 'Meeting Rudolf Steiner'

A note from the publisher

For more than a quarter of a century, **Temple Lodge Publishing** has made available new thought, ideas and research in the field of spiritual science.

Anthroposophy, as founded by Rudolf Steiner (1861-1925), is commonly known today through its practical applications, principally in education (Steiner-Waldorf schools) and agriculture (biodynamic food and wine). But behind this outer activity stands the core discipline of spiritual science, which continues to be developed and updated. True science can never be static and anthroposophy is living knowledge.

Our list features some of the best contemporary spiritual-scientific work available today, as well as introductory titles. So, visit us online at **www.templelodge.com** and join our emailing list for news on new titles.

If you feel like supporting our work, you can do so by buying our books or making a direct donation (we are a non-profit/charitable organisation).

office@templelodge.com

Numerous appreciations by Beckh's colleagues and his biographer; introducing the *Collected Works of Hermann Beckh.*

Festschrift: Essays in Honour of Hermann Beckh
English ed. Leominster: Anastasi 2016.
on the Centenary of *Buddha und seine Lehre* and the completion of the English translation *Buddha's Life and Teaching,* also
the transcription and translation of Beckh's *Das Geheimnis des musikalischen Schaffens: Der Mensch und die Music/ The Mystery of musical Creativity: The Human Being and Music* and the translation of Gundhild Kačer-Bock's biography *Hermann Beckh: Life and Work*

Further publications
The ongoing publication of the *Collected Works of Hermann Beckh* continues in 2018/19 and beyond. We are publishing in English everything available, including all articles, lectures, book reviews, appreciations, obituaries and unpublished material.

A German-English *Jahrbuch-Yearbook* is planned.
Please send all contributions for the *Yearbook,* on any aspect of Beckh's life and work: Indology, Christology, speech & language, music, *etc.* (preferably in Word or rtf format) to: alanstotty@gmail.com

Note:
We are desperately searching for copies of Hermann Beckh's music for The Act of Consecration of Man. Scores are held neither by the Archives of The Christian Community (Berlin), nor the Music Archives. Any possible leads would be most welcome (e-mail address above)—A. S. 2017.